I0558787

Conquer Through Surrender

Conquer Through Surrender

A Survival Guide to Overcoming
Life's Toughest Trials

Pete Robertson

Set Free Press

Published by Set Free Press
Copyright © 2024 by Pete Robertson

All rights reserved. No part of this book may be reproduced in any manner whatsoever without written permission except in the case of brief quotations embodied in critical articles and reviews. Requests for permission to reproduce should be addressed in writing to Set Free Press via email to permission@setfreepress.com.

First Printing, 2024

Printed in the United States of America

To order additional copies of this resource, you may order online at www.setfreepres.com.

Scripture quotations are taken from the Holy Bible, with different translations as indicated within the book and used by permission.

ISBN/SKU 979-8-9901733-2-3
EISBN 979-8-9901733-3-0

CONTENTS

Introduction

As Christians, we are called to navigate life with the grace and resilience exemplified by Jesus. However, life can be incredibly challenging. If we are honest with ourselves, we recognize that we are all imperfect, grappling with various issues. We worry, we fear, we indulge in harmful behaviors, and we struggle with vices. We swear, we lie, and we often fall short of the perfection we aspire to. Our lives can sometimes seem overwhelming, and we often find ourselves wrestling with areas where we know we should do better. We feel hopeless, even foolish, as we question why we can't seem to attain the joy and peace described in the Bible.

To be truly transformed and conquer our areas of inadequacy, we must be broken, contrite, and honest with ourselves. We are all, in a sense, hypocrites, lost and seeking a savior to rescue us from our own flaws.

There is hope, and Jesus is the perfect example for us to follow. He will guide and teach us how to live a fulfilling and impactful life. Despite facing incredibly challenging trials, just as we do, Jesus emerged victorious, living a pure and holy life that pleased God. He didn't just endure His trials—He taught us essential lessons on how to thrive even when life gets tough.

In John 17:21-24 Jesus prays that His disciples will all be one, just as He and the Father are one. He went on to say as you are in me, Father, and I am in you. And may they be in us so that the world will believe you sent me. "I have given them the glory you gave me, so they may be one as we are one. I am in them and you are in me. May they experience such perfect unity that the world will know that you sent me and that you love them as much as you love me. Father, I want these whom you have given me to be with me where I am. Then they can see all the glory you gave me because you loved me even before the world began!

By becoming one with Jesus, just as He is one with the Father, we gain the power and authority to overcome the trials we face and live victoriously, even in the midst of our troubles. This union empowers us to seek unity with Him, mirroring His unity with the Father. With His power, we are equipped to conquer life's battles.

A fitting Bible verse that reflects this is John 16:33 (NIV): "I have told you these things, so that in me you may have peace. In this world you will have trouble. But take heart! I have overcome the world." If Jesus overcame the world, we can too, because we are united with Him.

My vision for this book is to inspire a profound trust in, and fervent following of, Jesus across all facets of life. I long to see believers ablaze with passion for Christ—radically transformed and emboldened in their faith journey. This book aspires to awaken Christians to their calling as fervent warriors, championing a vibrant and dynamic faith. It is rooted in the biblical truth that we "Conquer Through Surrender", as expressed in 2 Corinthians 12:9, where the Lord declares, "My grace is sufficient for you, for my power is made perfect in weakness."

Through walking in the Spirit (Galatians 5:25), believers invite the divine power of God into their lives, enabling them to navigate and overcome life's challenges. This book aims to show that an intimate relationship with Jesus can fill your life with excitement and bring about continuous transformation. Reflecting Romans 12:2, which urges us not to conform to this world but to be transformed by the renewing of our minds, it highlights the profound changes that occur when we connect deeply with Him.

In essence, this work seeks to guide believers into an ever-deepening realization that a life intertwined with Jesus is anything but mundane—it is an adventure of faith, ever-evolving and marked by the triumphs of His kingdom.

This book aims to delve deeply into the heart of our Christian faith, anchoring us in the pivotal truth that Jesus is the Alpha and Omega of our existence—as declared in John 15:5, "apart from [Him] you can do nothing." It will explore how Jesus led a sanctified life and extend an invitation to us, His followers, to live in holy distinction from the world, empowered by His guiding hand.

Emphasizing that our underlying motives shape our thoughts and actions, the book will also guide us to examine and realign our intentions with the pure motives of Jesus. We'll discover that Jesus—fully human, yet divine—lived with an unwavering focus on glorifying God in every breath, every action, and every word. He modeled a life steeped in constant communion with the Father, a life where every act was an act of worship.

This narrative will serve as a reminder that we, too, are called to emulate Jesus' way of life, dedicating every moment to the praise and exaltation of God. Thus, this work is not just about learning values—it's about transforming our lives to mirror the purposeful and worshipful existence that Jesus so perfectly demonstrated.

This book will guide us through the challenging terrains of our Christian journey, particularly addressing the trials that are an inherent part of our walk with God. We will come to understand that these trials are not setbacks but beneficial trials, shaping us for the better, contrary to what many might believe. In the throes of difficulties, we are reassured that God is ever-present, diligently crafting a masterpiece within us, known only to Him.

Additionally, we will explore the concept of "living simply." This is a challenging notion in a world where abundance is often equated with success. To live a life of victorious surrender, embracing simplicity is essential. We will learn that while small adjustments can be delightful, it is the significant, sometimes disruptive changes that can be truly transformative. Our everyday habits and routines often clash with God's grand design for our lives.

Furthermore, we will recognize that each day presents uncounted opportunities to flourish and assert dominion for the glory of God. We will discover that a life dedicated to Jesus is one of continual action—whether in moments of quiet prayer or in the throng of life's battles. Living in step with Christ means our journey should pulse with vibrancy—never dull, always moving with purpose and intention.

Imagine a nation transformed by the same compassion that Christ showed for the lost. Picture the church, united, making monumental strides in sharing the love of God and reaching the lost with a message of hope and salvation.

As you journey through the pages of this book, my prayer is that you will gain profound insights into the essence of a life "Conquered Through Surrender"—a life that brings you into a closer relationship with God and emulates the exemplary life of self-giving that His Son demonstrated.

At the close of each chapter, you'll find a set of reflective talking points. These are designed to guide you through a personal reflection of the material you've just explored. They serve an equally powerful purpose in small group discussions, fostering a deeper conversation about the divine insights you've encountered. Engaging with these questions earnestly and with humility is a vital step in applying God's revelations to your life's journey. I earnestly encourage you to embrace this practice for your spiritual growth as you progress through the book.

Understanding Surrender

Jesus said in Luke 14:33 "So therefore, any one of you who does not renounce all that he has cannot be my disciple."

This opening chapter lays the groundwork for the central theme of this book: understanding and embodying a life conquered through the act of surrender. We will delve into a crucial question: What exactly must we surrender, and how do we go about it? Surrender, as defined by Webster's Dictionary, means "to yield to the power, control, or possession of another," and "to give up completely or agree to forgo especially in favor of another." This book will guide us in relinquishing our need for control, power, and possessions, entrusting them into the hands of Jesus.

Designed to furnish practical strategies, this book assists Christians in flourishing within their spiritual walk. By surrendering to Jesus, we access His power and wealth to be utilized for His Glory. We'll examine pathways to living daily in consummate triumph, addressing the stark reality that many Christians grapple with intermittent victories, often marred by feelings of depression or guilt.

Aiming to bring clarity to how we perceive Jesus, this book will empower believers to act in accordance with His power, bridging the gap between knowing what should be done and actual behavior. Readers will navigate through real-life scenarios common to us all, learning to interpret each event from God's perspective.

If this book has caught your eye, it's likely a whisper in your heart is seeking more of Jesus in your life, or you're navigating through life's challenges, searching for mastery but unsure of the path ahead. As the intriguing title sparked your curiosity, I extend a word of caution before you venture deeper into these pages. Embarking on this journey to conquer life via surrender demands a formidable price: the life you currently know. It requires an embrace of a transformation that, while challenging, promises to align with your highest good.

Throughout this book, you will encounter continuous invitations to forsake the helm of your personal desires, entrusting them instead to the aspirations Jesus holds for your existence. More than mere suggestions, these are appeals for profound sacrifices—to exchange your personal sentiments for the compassionate outlook of Jesus, to lay down every possession that strays from the divine blueprint crafted for you. Jesus himself articulated this stark requirement in Luke 14:33, stating, "So therefore, any one of you who does not renounce all that he has cannot be my disciple."

Confronted with this uncompromising truth, you may stand at a crossroads—a part of you considering retreat, another ignited by the challenge, eager to explore further. Regardless, I make you a promise. A life conquered through surrender is not only attainable but harbors an unparalleled richness beyond anything this world can provide. Believe me when I say the rewards of a life dedicated to Jesus eclipse all earthly offerings.

Many Christians are familiar with the promise of salvation and the joyous prospect of eternal life with Jesus in heaven. However, this assurance often resides in the future--so what does it mean to live for Jesus in the present moment, here on Earth? The question beckons: Is it possible to live victoriously for Jesus, harnessing His power to overcome daily challenges in every aspect of our lives?

The experiences of Christ's followers vary, some consistently walk in triumph while others grapple with defeat, feeling unheard by God amidst their pleas. The concept of wielding His power day-to-day can be overshadowed by persistent doubt and worry. I, too, have found myself in the quiet of the night, questioning God with a heavy heart, "Why?" I demanded answers, unable to understand His timing, His seeming indifference, and at the bleakest of times, doubted His goodness, perceiving His divine plan as harsh and uncaring.

This uncertainty, this worry, it shackled my ability to live fully in Jesus's empowering presence. My vision was clouded by the hope of heaven, yet I was immobilized, unable to fully engage in the abundant life Jesus offers us here and now.

Reflecting on my journey of faith, there have been times when I thought I had fully surrendered to God, pausing with bated breath for His divine intervention—only to find that His arrival wasn't aligning with my expectations. The waiting stretched on, endlessly it seemed, without a trace of God's presence. There were moments so bleak, that I questioned His very existence, and, feeling abandoned, I took matters into my own hands, scrambling for solutions to my own predicaments. Does this resonate with anyone?

Despite my turmoil, I maintained the rhythm of my religious life—attending church, and participating in various activities. There was a sense of duty in these actions, a sort of spiritual citizenship I thought I was upholding. The routines of faith brought me a temporary comfort, a semblance of fulfillment, but inside, I recognized a void. It seemed I was merely going through the motions, ticking off boxes on an unseen checklist. The problem? I was bereft of true power or victory in my life. All that remained were my efforts and the barren results they bore.

It was only later in my journey that a profound realization dawned upon me: I had misunderstood both the nature of Jesus and my purpose on Earth. This understanding forms the core of what this book aims to unfold. Here, we will discover that we are, as Romans 8:37 proclaims, "more than conquerors through Him who loved us." This text is dedicated to revealing how a follower of Christ is empowered to surmount worldly challenges and secure victory—echoing the assurance given in 1 John 5:4, "For everyone born of God overcomes the world. This is the victory that has overcome the world, even our faith."

However, stepping into this truth demands from us a surrender in humble obedience, allowing God to reign sovereignly over our lives. The path is strewn with difficulty and steeped in challenge, and yet, the fruits it yields are immeasurable. Attempting to encapsulate the utter exhilaration of a life wholly devoted to Jesus would be an endeavor in vain, for the experience is beyond the confines of language.

This book is crafted to speak to hearts across the spectrum of faith— from the seasoned Christian anchored in their journey with the Lord to the New Believer taking their first tentative steps. All are invited to embark on this transformative exploration.

In an inspiring edition of Decision Magazine, I stumbled upon an enlightening article by the renowned Billy Graham, a name synonymous with unwavering faith and evangelism. For those unfamiliar, Billy Graham was a vessel of divine purpose, whose life's work involved bringing the gospel's light to millions across the globe. His teachings and writings have been a cornerstone for many, including myself— I've frequently drawn upon his wisdom when crafting sermons for our community.

Billy Graham spoke of a concept that is both simple and profound: total surrender. As followers of Christ, the pursuit of conquering life through surrender requires a complete realignment with Jesus. Achieving this necessitates Jesus taking the helm in three crucial domains of our existence: the mind, the body, and our very will—our self-control.

The transformation within these spheres occurs when we, as believers, begin to perceive Jesus as He perceived His Father—through a lens of complete trust and unwavering obedience. It all boils down to an act of simple surrender.

This book is a guide, a roadmap to what surrendering these areas of our lives truly entails. However, before we delve deeper into that journey, let's first engage with Billy Graham's insights as he expounds on these three pivotal aspects of our lives with wisdom and clarity.

What is total Surrender?

Billy Graham said "If you want a change in your life, if you want forgiveness and peace and joy that you've never known before, God demands total surrender. He becomes the Lord and the ruler of your life. You're surrendering all the time. When I fly in an airplane and I sit down in the seat, I'm surrendering to that plane. Nothing I can do about it. I've been operated on several times, and I didn't negotiate with the doctors. As they took the knives out and put the anesthetic in, I put my full trust in those doctors that they were going to do the right thing. God said, "I know the plans I have for you, ... plans to prosper you and not to harm you, plans to give you hope and a future" (Jeremiah 29:11, NIV). That's what God says. He's not here to condemn you. He's here to bless you and love you and take you into His arms and say, "I forgive you. I'll change your life. And when you die, you will go to Heaven." That's what God is saying if you will surrender totally and completely. But you can't hold anything back."[i]

The insight is as clear as it is profound: nothing short of total surrender is required of us as followers of Jesus. Reflecting on my own spiritual walk, I realize that for the majority of my life as a Christian, I held back from this unconditional surrender. Clad in a veneer of righteousness and holiness, I comforted myself with the thought that human imperfection was inevitable and that God's grace would blanket my shortcomings.

Yet, I straddled two worlds – one anchored in the temporal allure of earthly existence and the other in my commitment to Christ, unwittingly crafting an illusion of piety for those around me, or so I believed. The truth I've come to recognize is how often we're oblivious to our own pride and the areas of our life where surrender has not been wholehearted. It is striking how easily we can be deceived into considering ourselves upright when, in reality, we fall short. Indeed, as Mark 10:18 reminds us, there is only One who is truly good, and that is Jesus.

This book aims to illuminate the parts of our lives where our surrender might be incomplete, and conversely, to acknowledge the aspects where we're thriving. It is my heartfelt prayer that through the Holy Spirit, the scales fall from our eyes, allowing us to perceive Jesus with unobstructed clarity and to be humbled, stripping away any vestige of pride.

What do we need to surrender?

It would be presumptuous of me to think that I could surpass the clarity with which Billy Graham speaks on the subject of surrender. Therefore, as I touched upon earlier, I would like to reiterate his profound insights into the three areas we must surrender to achieve true fulfillment.

The First need Billy Graham explores is that we need to surrender our minds.

"Now, when you surrender your mind to God, it means not only what we think but how we think. Some think that when you come to Christ, you have to leave your mind behind. Our faith is not irrational. Jesus will stand the inspection of any scientist, mathematician, or intellectual in the world. I read that by the time you reach college age, you will have seen more than 200,000 television commercials. Can you believe that? Congress debated what influence advertising was having on children's behavior. The average 21-year-old has seen 10,000 hours of violent programs. No wonder we have shootings in our schools. Our minds get saturated with violence or swearing or sex or whatever it is. A survey found that 77 percent of all allusions to sex on network television involve sex outside of marriage, and that cheapens love.

The Bible says, "You were taught, with regard to your former way of life, to put off your old self, which is being corrupted by its deceitful desires; to be made new" (Ephesians 4:22, 23, NIV). You can be made new. You see, your mind is more than a computer. In a computer, the programs don't get stronger the more you use them, but it's not true with what you see and hear. What is repeated is reinforced in our minds. What we remember influences what we do. The Bible says, "For as [a person thinks] in his heart, so is he" (Proverbs 23:7). What do you think in your heart? What are you really like down inside? Television also creates a problem or a dilemma and then in 30 minutes neatly resolves the problem, and the viewer enjoys a feeling of release. But that's not the way it is in real life. In real life, our problems won't go away rapidly. We're conditioned to want things immediately, right now: "I want gratification now. I want my way now." The Bible says, "Whatsoever things are true and honest and just and pure and lovely, think on these things" (Cf. Philippians 4:8). Is that what you think about? Good things? Or do you think about things you know are not right?

The Bible says, "You will keep him in perfect peace, whose mind"—your mind—"is stayed on You" (Isaiah 26:3). Get your mind on Christ every day, all day long because the devil is fighting for your soul. There are two forces at work inside of you. One is satanic, and one is God. Don't let the devil corrupt your mind. "Let this mind be in you which was also in Christ Jesus"[ii]

Bill Graham eloquently emphasized the profound connection between our minds and the daily situations we encounter. He insightfully pointed out that our mind acts as a reservoir; what we pour into it eventually flows out into our actions and words. Building on this premise, this book delves deep into the parts of our hearts that are deeply influenced by our thoughts. It will guide us on a journey to harness our thoughts, enabling us to flourish in each moment granted by God. Furthermore, we will uncover how our underlying motives shape the trajectories of our thoughts, sometimes leading us astray, and learn how to navigate paths that serve us better.

The second area that we will need to surrender according to Billy Graham is our Body.

He went on to say; "One of the great debates today is who owns the body. Doctors, lawyers, clergy, judges and juries debate the moral, ethical, and legal sides of this issue. And the questions surrounding suicide, euthanasia, and abortion center on the issues of who owns and controls your body. Who controls your body? The Bible says if you're a Christian, your body does not belong to you. It belongs to God. And the Bible also says that it's God's temple. Your body is God's temple, and He dwells in you if you really know Christ (see 1 Corinthians 3:16). Well, you say, "Billy, what do you think about sex?" I wouldn't be here if it weren't for sex, and you wouldn't be either. God created sex. He made us sexual human beings, men and women.

The scholar Eugene Kennedy wrote that sex is being used for a whole host of reasons for which it was never intended. And that's true. There's no such thing as free sex or free love. There's a price tag of broken relationships, broken hearts, broken bodies, and broken families. God created us as sexual beings. But from the beginning, God planned that the full expression of sex is to be within marriage. What about you? If you have or are living outside of God's original intention, you can ask God to forgive you, change you, and give you the power to resist every temptation. He'll do it. The Bible says, "Do not be deceived: Neither the sexually immoral nor idolaters nor adulterers ... will inherit the kingdom of God" (1 Corinthians 6:9, 10, NIV). In other words, you can't go to Heaven unless you get it cleared up. And the only way to get it cleared up is at the cross where the blood of Jesus Christ, His Son cleanses from all sin.

Jesus said, "[You] must be born again" (John 3:7). You can start all over with a new life. He'll forgive all the past and give you power for the future. Your heart can be changed. It's changed through prayer. It's changed by reading the Bible. It's changed by listening to the Holy Spirit. Everybody is tempted. The devil tempts everybody, every one of us. I've been tempted hundreds of times; so have you. Temptation is not sin. It's when you yield to temptation that it becomes sin. Christ died to give you a new heart and a new desire.[iii]

Like many, I too have placed my body in situations where it doesn't belong, echoing the wisdom of Billy Graham who once said, "The body is the temple that the Holy Spirit dwells in." As such, wherever our bodies travel, we are, in essence, carrying God with us. In the upcoming chapters, we'll examine the possibility that our lives may require various adjustments. These could range from reevaluating a current relationship to reconsidering our workplace environments. Recognizing and implementing these necessary changes is pivotal in mastering life's journey.

For some, these alterations might entail significant life overhauls; for others, only slight tweaks may be necessary. In my experience, I had to undertake both extensive and minor adjustments, which occurred frequently but were integral to my growth. Despite the challenges, the positive results I've witnessed are irreplaceable, and I wouldn't exchange them for anything.

As we venture through this book, I hope we can frequently pause for reflection and prayer, offering every part of ourselves to Jesus. My prayer is that we open ourselves to be reshaped by Him, to become more in His likeness. Let us embrace a posture of constant surrender to His will as we absorb the lessons on these pages.

The last area Billy Graham says that we need to surrender is our will, He went on to say:

> Before Jesus healed or helped people, He would normally say, "Will you? Are you willing?" And I'm asking you, will you surrender to Christ? Will you let Christ dominate your life and be the Lord of your life? Will you? That's the question He asks. The Scripture says, "Whosoever will, let him come" (see Revelation 22:17).

You say, "Lord, I will receive you into my heart tonight. Forgive me of my past, the things that I've done wrong. I want You to give me a new direction in my life. I want You to fill up this empty place in my life."

Have you ever surrendered yourself unconditionally to Christ? Have you ever given Him your mind and your body and your will? When you come to Christ, that's just the beginning because you must live for Him. And in living for Him, that means that the dominant feature of your life will be love. Whatever the color of someone's skin, you love them. You go out of your way to be friends with people of another race. That's how you love.

Billy Graham profoundly taught us about the necessity of yielding our will to Jesus. I refer to this act of will as "control," a concept that is often invisible to many Christians. Unaware of the areas they dominate, they are equally oblivious to what they ought to relinquish. Through my counseling, I have met Christians who see their spiritual journey as perfect, believing that they are immune to mistakes even when it is clear that they have a controlling lifestyle. I once felt this way and I had no idea that my vision was obscured by the pervasive control that I held in my life.

In this book, we will explore how to identify and understand this control within our everyday spirituality. It's imperative for us as Christians to perceive our lives through God's lens. Without this clarity, we risk dictating our fate while mistakenly believing we are aligning with God's will. Unlike the world, which operates constrained by time and claims omniscience, Jesus transcends time and possesses true foresight. The world, limited by its temporal scope and despite its boldness, stands in stark contrast to the profound wisdom of Christ. **It is within this contrast that we must learn to navigate, recognize our control, and learn to surrender it to the One who sees beyond the bounds of our temporal existence.**

As followers of Jesus, we are called to be present in the world while not adopting its values (John 17:14). Our mission is not to emulate worldly behaviors but to live in sync with Jesus, adopting the rhythm of His ways. For those of us who are new believers, this shift in lifestyle is a process that involves learning and growth. At times, we may inadvertently make choices that resemble worldly ones, reflecting our ongoing development.

Being immersed in the world can sometimes lead us to act without wisdom. Yet, in Christ, we are embraced by grace—a grace that nurtures our growth and spares us from condemnation. The world often expects perfection and is quick to condemn, but in Christ, we find patience and understanding.

Sheep are often used as a metaphor for us for a specific reason—they're known for their lack of understanding. In calling us His sheep, God doesn't insult our intelligence but rather points to our need for guidance. Apart from Jesus, who is our ultimate truth, we lack the wisdom to navigate life effectively (John 15:5). Just as sheep without a shepherd can stray into danger, we too need the vigilant care of our Shepherd.

Through total surrender to Jesus, we protect ourselves from the harsh judgments of the world and find solace in His love. It's in this relationship that we are transformed and gradually reshaped in His likeness, free from the weight of condemnation and guided by His gentle hand.

To embrace the transformative journey with God, we must first acknowledge that our pride and need for control require the refinement of God's grace. It's a humbling lesson to accept that our own understanding falls short in comparison to God's perfect wisdom. We must come to realize that our existence is not about elevating ourselves, but is wholly centered on glorifying Jesus. To believe otherwise is to be deceived by falsehoods that do not originate from God but from the adversary, Satan.

The purpose of this book is to steer us towards seeing our lives through God's eyes, an outlook that releases us into the liberating promise of God's truth. By doing so, our lives undergo a profound transformation. Our perception and awareness are renewed, enabling us to view the world in a light that aligns with divine truth.

A life surrendered to God resembles the life of Jesus—it radiates peace, joy, and purpose. It's a victorious life in the spiritual realm, one that subdues the enemy at every turn. As Christians, we've been gifted a new life by God, and with the aid of this book—firmly rooted in Biblical teachings—we can learn to navigate and flourish in our spiritual journey to the fullest extent.

Having delved into the concept of total surrender, our next step is to explore the significant role of motives in our daily decision-making. Discerning whether our underlying intentions align with God's desires is crucial. In the upcoming chapter, we'll unravel the importance of this alignment and understand why motives that diverge from God's can impact the course of our spiritual journey.

Understanding SURRENDER
Talking Points

1. What are your expectations from this book?

2. Have you ever questioned God about why you're experiencing certain challenges? What insights has He given you? Please explain.

3. What does it mean to achieve total surrender?

4. How can we surrender our minds?

5. In what ways can we surrender our bodies?

6. How do we let go of our will or control?

2

Why My Motives Matter

In sharing my story, I aim to offer you, the reader, a window into my past and the driving forces that shaped my journey. Often, we remain unaware of how our misguided motives—those not in alignment with God's will—can lead us down paths He never intended for us to tread. This realization came to me when God grasped my heart and unveiled the real motivations behind my actions. He undertook a profound transformation within me, stripping away an identity founded on anything but Him.

Here's the profound truth: I believed I was acting under God's motivation, living life in accordance with His desires. Yet, for a considerable part of my life, I was ensnared by a deception—I let worldly concerns steer me instead of God's truth. My perspective of God was skewed, and this led me down barren paths. My personal transformation doesn't mean God will work in you in the same way, but He may need to cleanse you of a worldly identity to bestow upon you His divine image, a process He graciously guided me through.

If you've already endured this profound shedding of your old self and are being remade in God's likeness, you'll find resonance with the experiences I share. Conversely, if you haven't encountered such a transformation, the insights in this book may stir a sense of unrest in your heart. My prayer is that you won't be disquieted but will continue to engage with my story. Over the years, God has revealed to me His boundless love and perfect understanding of what is best for us. He desires only the most excellent outcomes for each of us—a divine touch that enhances our earthly efforts beyond comparison.

Raised in a Christian home, the desire to know and serve God was instilled in me from the beginning. Yet, like many, I found that it was I who helmed the course of my life, not God. Reflecting on my past, the pattern of God's presence is unmistakably woven throughout the tapestry of my decisions. It's now apparent why I made certain choices and why my behaviors took shape as they did.

From an early age, an inner fire propelled me to aspire towards significance. My nature has always been resilient, laser-focused, and ambitious. Along my journey, I've been blessed to encounter individuals who, with divine orchestration, profoundly influenced my thoughts and steered my life's direction.

As you delve into the pages of my story, I encourage you to ponder the influences in your own life. Consider who or what has shaped your actions and decisions. This introspection is crucial, as it uncovers the driving forces behind your motivations—revealing whether you stand in a place of surrender to God or to your own desires. Your answer to this question is a pivotal one, as it anchors your heart's true allegiance.

My life has been profoundly shaped by the unwavering motivation of several key individuals. Foremost among them are my parents. Raised in a devout Christian household, they instilled in me the dual virtues of fearing God and embracing hard work.

In addition to my parents' foundational influence, my high school baseball coach played a pivotal role in my development. His relentless approach aimed to not only break me down but more importantly, to build me into the finest pitcher I could become. He instilled in me a powerful mantra: "Quitting is not an option. Make it happen." This ethos of perseverance was complemented by a recognition of the unavoidable rigor of life's journey – a concept that he championed with the warning that shying away from it was equal to accepting failure. Admittedly, he also imparted some lessons that were less than divine, which I choose to remember with a light-hearted chuckle rather than vocalize.

Another significant figure in my life has been my uncle. His entrepreneurial spirit has been evident throughout his successful business career, a path that I found myself reflecting upon frequently during my business endeavors. His demonstrated attributes of leadership, success, and the connotations of affluence provided me with a tangible blueprint for my aspirations.

While not all influences have been entirely positive, even the skepticism of my father-in-law has inadvertently molded my ambition. Meeting his doubts about my business acumen with a steadfast resolve, I turned his disbelief into a catalyst for my relentless drive, transforming years of upset into fuel for my pursuits.

Moreover, my spiritual journey has had its detours, and inevitably, straying from my faith had a ripple effect on my decisions. This detour, in hindsight, also shaped the person I am today, underscoring the complex tapestry of motivation that life offers.

Reflecting on the past, I now recognize how God has used each of these influential individuals to motivate me in various ways. Each has left a distinct imprint on my life, contributing both positive and negative elements to my story. In the following chapter, I intend to delve more into the negative motivations, unravelling how those darker influences not only served to misguide me towards glorifying lesser ideals, but also spurred my decision to seize control of my life rather than allowing God to steer my path.

As I peer into the recesses of my past, I understand the root of my hunger for education. My parents, who placed little emphasis on formal learning and lacked extensive education themselves, inadvertently catalyzed my drive. I rationalized from an early age that whether I was to run a business or assume the mantle of a Pastor, education would be pivotal. This realization ignited within me a relentless thirst for knowledge. It became the very fuel I used to push myself, the momentum that drove me to constantly read and study any material within my reach.

My coach would often say that things happen only when we take the initiative to make them happen. This doctrine was deeply ingrained in us as athletes. However, with the wisdom of hindsight, I now see that this philosophy doesn't align with my faith. In truth, it's God who initiates, and my role is to follow His lead—not the reverse.

Despite my deep love and respect for my uncle, I recognize that my overbearing pride led me to view my relationship with him through the lens of competition. I was determined to surpass his success, seeing it as a challenge I was compelled to win at any cost. This misplaced competitive spirit was misguided, a realization that underscores a deeper reflection on my motivations.

My father-in-law's skepticism and lack of support also played a significant role in shaping my trajectory. I became obsessed with disproving his doubts, eager to one day flaunt my achievements. Looking back, I can see that each decision I made sprung from my own desires and what I presumed to be best for me.

These choices were steered by my ambition to carve my own path, serving as my own guide, all the while masquerading these actions as divinely inspired. It was pride that fueled this delusion, a pride that sought to elevate myself to the role of a creator in my life rather than a follower of God's will.

Consequences of Choices

My motivations set the compass for my life's journey, but regrettably, I rarely paused to consider the fallout of my decisions. Reminiscent of Newton's third law—which posits that every action has an equal and opposite reaction—I've come to understand that my decisions, made independently of God's guidance, often resulted in pain and struggle.

As I reflect on the past, it becomes clear that my temperament was consistently marked by moodiness, a demanding nature, and a compulsion to exert control. Such traits are not uncommon among those of us with type-A personalities, but they made me difficult to be around, particularly when I was single-mindedly pursuing a goal or attempting to prove a point. The wake of my journey was cluttered with the remnants of bridges I had callously burnt, unconcerned about the harm done. I perceived others as lesser, failing to see them as God's precious creations meant to be cherished. My recklessness knew no bounds, as I was perpetually chasing the next dollar or attempting to dominate the next individual, far removed from the grace with which God operates, especially in His treatment of people.

The most profound cost of my behavior was the toll it took on my family. My wife and children bore the brunt of a life led by impulse, not spirit; they were raised in a household overshadowed by a harsh tone and an oppressive regime. In a particularly stark declaration, I remember insisting that within the walls of my home, democracy was non-existent; it was a dictatorship ruled by my edicts—my way or the highway. This environment, I now see, was the antithesis of the nurturing and loving atmosphere I should have cultivated.

If you were to ask my family about the life we shared, they might acknowledge the hard times but still describe me as a "cool guy" who loved them deeply. My adeptness at straddling the line between worldliness and godliness was a performance; I became skilled at concealing my true emotions and presenting an image of normalcy. My active involvement in the church and on mission trips, alongside my generous tithing and offerings, bolstered my self-image as a "good guy," and through His Grace, I remained God's child despite my duplicity.

Upon introspection, the issue lay within my motives, which seldom aligned with God's will, restricting me from fully immersing myself in His grace due to my need for control and hesitancy to place my unwavering trust in Him. The shadows from my past dodged the illuminating light of Christ, allowing them to be manipulated for lesser means more often than I'd like to admit. Enshrouded in my self-justification, I misconstrued my actions as aligned with God's wishes. For a long time, the thought of living differently was incomprehensible to me, stunted by my stubbornness and decisiveness.

Motivated by self-determined ideals of what I considered best for my life, I rarely paused to truly inquire about God's perspective. Although I professed complete surrender to His will, in reality, it was lip service devoid of genuine submission. There were moments when I sought God's guidance, but even then, my heart wasn't in a state of pure seeking; I asked without making space to listen, to be still, and to receive. All my actions revolved around self-interest, with little regard for others, save for when I stood to gain an advantage.

As a man, it's difficult to acknowledge these truths, but liberation has come through this confession. I had to confront my past, to be open and honest, to finally experience the transformation and freedom I longed for.

When God allowed Circumstances
to Rock My World

One day, my entire world fell apart. This was my come-to-Jesus moment, where God finally broke through the thick walls of my pride. It was 2008, marking the beginning of the end of Pete as I knew him. In His grace, God began to slowly open my eyes, revealing just how evil and controlling I had been. He showed me why I was driven by my own motives and where that control was leading me. Gradually, He began to share His purpose and plan for my life, stripping away everything that had kept me from Him.

The journey was beyond intense; God completely dismantled my identity. Everything I had grown up knowing and believing had to be relearned. He started replacing my misguided ways with His wisdom, love, and grace. It's amazing what happens when your life is no longer at the top and great suffering becomes your new normal. During my fall, I noticed that close friends and family members began treating me differently. Although I am not entirely sure why, I believe that as God was working in my life, I experienced a distance from others and a strong oppression that felt impossible to shake.

I realized this oppression stemmed from all the evil that had been controlling me. I remember crying out to God daily, hoping He would take this great trial from me, but it seemed as if my pleas fell on deaf ears. I recall many long hours of desperate prayer, pleading with God to hear me and change my circumstances, only to wake up the next morning to the same utter chaos.

I was unquestionably in the midst of the refiner's fire. As it says in Malachi 3:3 (NLT), *"He will sit like a refiner of silver, burning away the dross. He will purify the Levites, refining them like gold and silver, so that they may once again offer acceptable sacrifices to the LORD."* This scripture became a vivid reality for me as God worked to burn away my impurities, refining and transforming me through the trials.

This transformative experience felt like it lasted an eternity. I remember meeting with family and friends, hoping for encouragement, prayer, or some sort of relief. Instead, it felt like they were treating me like Job, offering their advice or opinions on what "I should do" or "how I should feel." It seemed as if they assumed my suffering was due to some sin in my life.

This was the first time in my life that I can honestly say I was waiting on God. I was alone, waiting, listening, praying, and seeking His direction. My family and friends repeatedly reminded me of how bad a person I was in the past. While I agreed that I had made poor choices before, that wasn't how Jesus saw me now. It hurt deeply that they couldn't see me as I now understood Jesus did.

Later, I discovered this is a tactic Satan uses to divert our focus from Jesus to our circumstances. I will delve more into this in the "Engage the Enemy" chapter. Despite my family's and friends' well-meaning but misguided interventions, they couldn't see how my world had completely shattered for God's sake, not my own. They missed the great and mighty work God was doing within me. Their inability to recognize what was happening during this initial stage of transformation hurt deeply and caused me to withdraw from them.

I felt so isolated and began to cast blame on each of them, convinced in my heart that their faith was so small and their legalistic outlook so wrong. I was a mess and couldn't understand why I harbored so much bitterness and hate inside. I remember asking God to help me love my family and others the way He does.

I went through times of deep depression where thoughts of suicide often crossed my mind. In fact, I had a close friend who was going through a similar process of being stripped down and, tragically, he did commit suicide. This devastated me completely and drove me to draw even nearer to God. I recall echoing Job's words from Job 10:1-7, questioning, "Why, God, are you doing this to me?" This deepened my desperation, yet also my reliance on God during one of the most challenging periods of my life.

> *Job 10:1-7 NIV "I loathe my very life; therefore I will give free rein to my complaint and speak out in the bitterness of my soul. I say to God: Do not declare me guilty, but tell me what charges you have against me. Does it please you to oppress me, to spurn the work of your hands, while you smile on the plans of the wicked? Do you have eyes of flesh? Do you see as a mortal sees? Are your days like those of a mortal or your years like those of a strong man, that you must search out my faults and probe after my sin. Though you know that I am not guilty and that no one can rescue me from your hand?"*

I was doing my best to walk Holy before God by allowing Him to strip me of the things in me that were not pleasing to Him. I just did not want to go through the hell I was experiencing. I am sure Job was thinking the same thing. The word fun would never have been used to describe this time of anguish.

Throughout my life, I navigated considerable trials without a firm grasp on faith or hope in God; indeed, understanding that such adversity could serve our greater good seemed an insurmountable concept. I admit there were moments when non-existence felt preferable to the sufferings I endured. Yet, it is often in our deepest anguish that extraordinary transformation occurs. In the throes of profound despair, as I approached the brink of my own limitations, I encountered the divine presence. In those silent, raw moments, God was with me, meticulously peeling away the layers of callousness that I had normalized within my soul.

It was then that I began to peel my eyes open, gaining insights into the profound truth encapsulated in Galatians 2:20: "I have been crucified with Christ and it is no longer I who live, but Christ lives in me." The lesson was clear; life presents a tapestry of varying seasons, and within each, God's presence is intricately woven, even if I was oblivious to it at the time. I had been a lifelong follower of Christ without ever surrendering to His sovereignty. A casual Christian, tepid in faith, I embodied the warning in Revelation 3:16, where lukewarm believers are admonished for their indifference.

However, my story does not conclude in mediocrity. For through these experiences, I have come to recognize the boundlessness of God's grace. His desire for us extends beyond lukewarm existence; His grace is not just a remedy but the very essence of a renewed life pulsing with fervent devotion. It's a graceful awakening to the reality that God's infallible grace is indeed sufficient for us all.

The Insane Thing God Asked Me To Do

Reaching the end of our own limits offers a profound opportunity for transformation. It is in this space of surrender that we are finally open to the divine whispers often drowned out by life's frenetic pace. Stillness before God becomes the conduit through which His voice is discerned.

This truth resonated within me in an unexpected sanctuary: my garage. There, on bended knee amidst tears and prayer, the still, small voice of God broke through my chaos. "Be still and wait on me," He urged. In my heart, I believed I had been doing just that, yet God was preparing me for a deeper level of trust.

It became clear that my approach to financial success, driven by my own hands, was in fact a shackle. God's message was unmistakable: "Trust in Me for your provision." My immediate response—a perplexed

"How?"—was met with divine assurance. "Cease your pursuit; I will guide opportunity to your door."

The narrative of the Israelites in the wilderness then cascaded into my thoughts, a poignant reminder of Jehovah Jireh, our Provider. The manna from heaven was not just physical sustenance; it was a testament to reliance on God's unerring provision.

Picture it: You are the provider for your family, and suddenly, you sense God's directive to halt all pursuit, to engage solely in worship, and to act only upon His command. It's a monumental shift from self-reliance to a deep-rooted faith in God's sovereignty—a radical call to obedience that echoes through the mundane and the miraculous moments of our lives.

Confronted with such a divine imperative, fear laced my initial reaction, accompanied by a whirlwind of doubts and questions. How would you react? For me, the thought of explaining this celestial directive to my family—my wife, my children—was met with trepidation. I could almost hear the incredulous responses of friends and loved ones, their voices tinged with skepticism, echoing the same disbelief that would frequently haunt my own thoughts.

I'll confess, this new path felt like a tightrope walk above an abyss of uncertainty. My conversations with God were no silent prayers but vocal, impassioned pleas for clarity and confirmation, often charged with the frustration of a man teetering on the edge of reason.

Yet, as days turned into weeks, a quiet transformation unfolded. My faith, rather than withering under the scrutiny and trials, began to deepen. Amid my fervor and turmoil, an inexplicable peace emerged as the presence of Jesus became more palpable, His love more profound than ever before. It dawned on me that God's hand was indeed at work, that His plans were unfurling with purpose—and that my sanity was intact.

Embracing this journey, I learned a fundamental truth: God's provision was not only a promise but a tangible reality. Worry lost its grip as I realized that in Him, everything is restored, and His timing is impeccably aligned with our needs. As trust supplanted anxiety, I witnessed the beauty of surrender, the assurance that in His hands, all things are made right.

Indeed, God's timing is impeccably perfect! Grasping the full extent of this concept has been a lengthy journey for me, one that I am still traversing. From my limited perspective, God seemed to operate on a timeline that defied my understanding of punctuality. His interventions often appeared untimely and bewildering, never conforming to expected patterns or conventional wisdom. It was as if He reveled in the art of surprise, weaving His divine purpose through a tapestry of ever-changing methods and scenarios.

Embracing this unpredictable rhythm, I discovered joy in the act of waiting on God. It became a delightful game, one where anticipation built with each unforeseen move of the Divine Maestro. I adopted a child-like stance of expectancy, eagerly looking forward to 'Papa's' next reveal with wonder and exhilaration.

For someone accustomed to the captain's seat—master of my daily existence—this surrender to God's commanding lead was nothing short of miraculous. Letting go and entrusting everything to Him is a feat that defies human capability, achievable only through His empowering presence.

The essence of faith, it seems, can sometimes demand a radical trust that borders on the incomprehensible. Consider, if you will, being asked by God to approach your employer with a request to forgo your salary, placing your financial needs wholly in divine hands. Such a proposition defies logic, it defies convention, and it certainly challenges our deeply ingrained instincts for self-preservation and security. This scenario parallels the profound request God placed upon me: to operate entirely under His guidance, refraining from action until His signal.

This might sound outlandish, but it reflects a broader spiritual mandate. It's not necessarily a literal call to reject compensation for our labor. Instead, it signifies a deeper call to entire surrender—that which controls us and that which we attempt to control. God beckons not just for a relinquishment of our constructs of security but for a wholesale renaissance of our lives.

In the pursuit of divine transformation, we're invited to abandon our old paradigms, our self-made blueprints of logic, and our illusion of control. It is an invitation to be reborn, to let go of the familiar and embrace the renewal that only He can orchestrate—a new creation in alignment with His perfect design and purpose.

Embracing God's direction and tackling the formidable tasks He sets before us manifests uniquely for everyone. It may require yielding control in areas of our lives that we hold especially dear. The truth is, relinquishing total control to God is not straightforward, and I suspect that many—like myself in the past—are under the illusion of surrender when, in fact, we maintain a tight grip on the reins.

Here is a test I have found to help determine if I have surrendered control over to God or not. When a trial comes, do you find yourself shaken, worried, stressed, or frustrated? Are you able to cast the situation over to God immediately, or do you wrestle with the problem and try to fix it yourself? The testing of our faith reveals where we stand in our relationship with God. Ultimately, we aim to harbor the fullness of Christ within us, which brings immense joy despite our trials. Life is not an uninterrupted sequence of perfect, effortless days. There are moments when joy is replaced by the need to weep, and that's perfectly natural.

Nonetheless, prompt yourself to reflect on this: Is there a deep, un-utterable joy that threads through your days, or do you find your mood fluctuating—bright on some days, darkened on others? I've come to rec-ognize that my own erratic sense of joy is an indicator of my reluctance to fully entrust my life to God's care. True peace and consistent joy are found when I stop piloting my path and rest entirely in the assurance of His embrace.

Reflecting on my journey, I've recognized a transformative shift in motives. Initially, my aspirations were the driving force, with God cast in the role of a supportive ally rather than the guiding force. This misalignment prevented me from fully grasping the essence of life post-conversion—it was not to be centered on me, but rather wholly on Him.

My inability to surrender to His leadership barred me from experi-encing the kind of exuberant joy the Bible talks about in James 1:2-4 *"Count it all joy, my brothers, when you meet trials of various kinds, for you know that the testing of your faith produces steadfastness. And let steadfastness have its full effect, that you may be perfect and complete, lacking in nothing."*

My decisions were influenced by my desires, overshadowing God's perfect will for me to lack nothing. It was a profound awakening, facili-tated by God's gentle revelation, that illuminated the discordance of my motivations with His divine purpose.

This epiphany was key in reshaping my worldview, allowing me to adopt His perspective gradually. Though the process was accompanied by discomfort, it was evident that even amid my distress, God's work was incessantly unfolding. He patiently schooled me in the art of looking beyond the veil of my circumstances to witness life through His eyes—thus beginning the true dance of joy in harmony with His unerring rhythm.

Consider this scenario, which illustrates the difference between having motives centered around "Self-Seeking motive" versus seeing things the way God would want. With a "God-seeking motive," here's how a typical doctor's visit might unfold:

"Self-Seeking Motive"

Reluctantly, I decide to go to the doctor because of a persistent ailment. Frustration builds as I think about needing to get better. Waiting in the lobby, I start to notice the time drag on, becoming increasingly aware that the doctor is taking much too long. Impatience and restlessness set in, but I convince myself to hold on a little longer.

Glancing around the waiting room, I wonder about the ailments of others, hoping not to catch anything from them. Trying to distract myself, I focus on the TV playing some random program, adding to my frustration with the thought of possibly getting even sicker. My name is finally called, and I rush to see the nurse. I am then ushered into another room, only to wait again.

After about another half hour, the doctor finally arrives. I quickly share all my symptoms, and after a series of brief questions, my appointment is over in a few minutes. Leaving the clinic, I head to CVS to get my prescription filled. I impatiently wait in line yet again and finally make my way home.

Does this sound familiar? While individual experiences may vary, this pretty much captures a common scenario for many of us.

"God-Seeking Motive"

With the right motives centered around God's will, my perspective on a doctor's visit has completely transformed. I now understand that it's not just about me; it's an opportunity to see and serve others through God's eyes.

Knowing that God is in control, I embrace my role as His ambassador, seeking chances to bless and pray for those I encounter. I see each person as someone deeply loved by God and make myself available to them, guided by the Holy Spirit. This could mean offering a gentle smile, holding a door open, letting someone go ahead of me, praying silently for others, or offering up my seat.

While it's true that there are times when we're too ill to think about others, kindness is always within our reach. Even in our sickness, we can still pray for someone or offer a small act of kindness. The point is, God is aware of everything happening in our lives. Our purpose remains to bring Him glory and draw closer to Him.

How do we know that this illness isn't part of a greater purpose? Perhaps God has placed us in this situation because we're the perfect person to speak to someone else in the waiting room at that precise moment. Focusing solely on my own motives makes me lose sight of God's higher plan and quench the Spirit in the process.

My trials have brought me to the foot of the cross, revealing that Jesus is my only true passion and motivation. Through my hardships, God has shown me my great intrinsic value and revealed His purpose and will for my life. Each trial has opened my eyes and pointed me to the cross, where I experience an indescribable love from Him—one that words cannot fully capture.

Now, I understand that I am to wait on Him and use all the talents and gifts He has given me to point others to the same Jesus I now love completely. In the past, my motivation was guided by what I believed was best for me. Influenced by the people around me and my life circumstances, I charted my path based on my own truth. I never considered my motivations from God's perspective or how they aligned with His word.

It was only through experiencing great heartache that God allowed me to identify my misguided motivations. By His grace, I have been able to replace them with the right motivations, aligned with His will and purpose for my life.

Now, my deepest motivation is to please God in everything I do. This shift in motivation was not easy for me to grasp without the help of the Holy Spirit.

I encourage you to ask God to reveal to you your own motivations and reflect on the direction your life has taken. Is your life aimed at bringing glory to God in everything, or is it driven by something else?

In the next chapter, we will explore the contrast between self-seeking motives and God-seeking motives. We will examine how these motivations influence our decision-making in every aspect of our lives, helping us to better understand the impact of our intentions.

Why MY MOTIVES Matter

Talking Points

1. Take a moment to pray and seek the Lord's guidance on this question: What has motivated you throughout your life, and are your current motives truly aligned with where Christ wants you to be?

2. Reflect on how God has shown you the way your motivations have directed the path you've taken in life.

3. Read Malachi 3:3- What does the concept of going through the refiner's fire mean to you personally?

4. Read Revelations 3:16 and answer the following questions:
   (a) To what is Jesus referring to in this verse?

   (b) Do you consider yourself to be a lukewarm Christian? Why or why not?

5. Share a time when you were a lukewarm Christian and how did God open your eyes to see this?

6. Read Galatians 2:20. Explain what this verse means to you.

7. What does it mean to be crucified with Christ daily?

8. Has God ever asked you to do something really challenging that required you to trust Him completely? Share your experience.

3

Motives: Self-Seeking Vs God-Seeking

"When you ask, you do not receive, because you ask with wrong motives, that you may spend what you get on your pleasures" James 4:3

Countless books and articles delve into the topic of motivation, emphasizing its fundamental influence on our life's trajectory. In the preceding chapter, I offered a glimpse into my personal story, sharing the pivotal motivators that shaped the course I elected to embark upon. My drive was fueled by an insatiable yearning for self-love, independence, and determination, a quest that was undeniably self-serving. This pursuit led me through a tumultuous journey rife with anguish, where solace eluded me—until I found my personal relationship with Jesus.

By no means do I profess to be an authority on the intricate workings of human motivation. My insights are drawn from lived experiences, contrasting a life propelled by self-serving motivations against one driven by the desire to live for Jesus. The transition from a self-centered existence to yielding to a calling by God has been transformational. In Jesus, I encounter daily victories, no longer as a combatant, but as one who conquers life challenges through surrender.

The essence of this book is to guide us towards seeing life through Jesus' lens. It prompts us to scrutinize our motivations, which are determinants of whether we will navigate life as victors, claiming daily triumphs, or not. The call is to assess not just what moves us, but also where it is moving us toward, establishing a foundation for a truly conquering life.

Lou Holtz once insightfully observed, "Your ability is what you're capable of doing. Motivation determines what you do. Attitude determines how well you do it." This aligns with the biblical passage in Matthew 25:15, where Jesus imparts talents to his disciples for their successful journey. Aligning with this, our abilities, as endowed by Jesus, are foundational—without them, as reiterated in John 15:5, we can accomplish nothing of lasting value.

In the previous chapter, I reflected on how my motivation rooted in a selfish desire to affirm my own significance led me astray, obscuring God's perfect will. This relentless drive to prove myself only served to veil the true essence of success. My personal journey revealed the critical impact our motivations have in shaping our lives. As Holtz mentions, our attitude—the lens through which we view our endeavors—can significantly amplify our efforts.

Admittedly, my attitude, when permeated by worldly desires, was one of unyielding determination. Yet, such a mindset, while initially propelling me forward, ultimately imposed a burdensome weight. This single-minded pursuit began to crumble, adversely influencing not just my well-being, but also those around me, as frustration and anger took root when success proved elusive.

At face value, Holtz's adage, through a worldly lens, portrays a life steeped in potential and accomplishment. Nonetheless, the stark truth emerges that any pursuit, if not anchored in Jesus as our central motivation, is destined to fall short. Without aligning our ambitions with the calling God gives us, we may find that the outcomes, however impressive they might initially appear, ultimately prove hollow and unsatisfying.

We were not created to shoulder the full weight of our responsibilities by ourselves. Our very creation was designed to have daily communion with our Father, entrusting Him with our worries and burdens (1 Peter 5:7). He is built to bear the brunt of our load, leaving us to tread lightly in His wake, serving joyfully at His behest. If our motivations draw us away from this divine service, then the weight of the world—our daily decisions, life's stresses, work demands, and family dynamics—becomes ours to bear.

As I shared in the previous chapter, my personal pursuit of fame and fortune was such a burden. It was a load I bore for too long, leading only to pain and ultimately failure. In order to fully understand Jesus and see Him as He wants to be seen, it is important to ask ourselves a critical question: What motivates us? Is it the allure of fame, the security of wealth, the bond of family, or the recognition of our peers?

These questions demand our candid introspection if we aspire to foster an intimate connection with Jesus. Without such honesty, our vision of Him is obscured. God's nature is unyieldly and exclusive in His devotion; He does not vie for our attention against the distractions and idols in our lives (Exodus 34:14). He patiently waits for us to lay down our armors of self-reliance and worldly pursuits.

Blinded by our own desires, we miss the evidences of His goodness and the best intentions He has for us. As declared in Romans 8:31, "If God is for us, who can be against us?" To live propelled by selfish aspirations prevents us from recognizing the depths of God's love. It is only when we relinquish these drives and embrace His divine motivation that we can fully appreciate His unwavering support and love for us.

This chapter is dedicated to outlining the stark differences between the motivations of the secular world and the transformative experience of yielding to Jesus. As previously mentioned, my past motivations were deeply rooted in self-love, self-reliance, self-determination, and a relentless quest for self-satisfaction. However, my perspective shifted dramatically when I relinquished these worldly drives and let Jesus become my guiding force.

In doing so, Jesus infused me with His attributes: self-love was replaced by a love for others, self-dependence transformed into a trust in God's sovereignty, self-will evolved into submission to God's will, and my self-seeking nature was reformed into a life of self-denial, taking up my cross to follow Him.

I was once misled by the world's definition of success, letting those hollow standards shape my aspirations. Now, let us explore these contrasts in depth, examining them through the lens of the Bible to gain a clearer, more divine understanding of what should drive our existence.

Our first motive contrast:
SELF-LOVE VERSUS LOVE FOR OTHERS

The quotes from singer Christina Perri and actress Lucille Ball underscore a prevailing sentiment in today's world about the importance of self-love as a prerequisite for success and healthy relationships. Perri suggests that only by loving ourselves wholeheartedly can we truly love others[iv], while Ball proposes that self-love aligns the rest of our lives[v]. Yet, these statements beg deeper scrutiny in the face of extreme adversities.

Can self-love truly prepare us to offer love to someone who has caused us unimaginable grief, such as the loss of a child? Within the confines of worldly logic, this seems implausible, but through the lens of Jesus' teachings, such profound forgiveness and love become possible.

The question posed by Ball's accepted truth is equally thought-provoking: Does prioritizing self-love indeed empower us to accomplish 'anything' in this world? What does this 'anything' refer to, and how far does the power of self-love extend in the face of circumstances that strip away control, such as a hostile takeover? The limitations of self-love as a sole motivating force are starkly visible here.

These reflections bring us to the heart of the matter: motivation. If our motivation is anchored solely in our self-love, how do we respond when it is abruptly halted by events beyond our grasp? Can a robust sense of self-sufficiency still guide us through? Or might we discover that a focus on self-love is not the cure-all we assumed it to be? The perspective of achieving everything by the sheer force of self-belief is challenged when we consider that our personal goals might not encompass the vastness of life's unpredictable nature.

In the end, these musings prompt us to contemplate whether there's a dimension of motivation beyond our own self-love—a motivation that's not easily shaken by the world's tribulations and instead offers a more resilient foundation for both personal achievement and the capacity to love others, even in the most trying circumstances.

In a world saturated with self-improvement literature and the mantra of self-love, it's easy to get swept up in the ideology that prioritizing one-self is the path to fulfillment. However, through my own experience, I've learned the limitations of such a belief system.

True love, the kind that fills and satisfies, extends beyond self.

As 1 John 4:16-19 articulates, understanding love begins with God:

> *"And so we know and rely on the love God has for us. God is love. Whoever lives in love lives in God, and God in them. In this way, love is made complete among us so that we can have confidence on the day of judgment because in this world we are like Jesus. There is no fear in love. But perfect love drives out fear, because fear has to do with punishment.*

The one who fears is not made perfect in love. We love because He first loved us."

This passage illuminates that to truly embrace love, we must recognize its source: God's enduring love for us. Self-love, when positioned as the pinnacle, falls short of the transformative love God intends. It is only when we prioritize loving God and acknowledging His love for us that we can fully appreciate and give love. In His love, we find completeness and security, shaping us into beings capable of loving others unapologetically and without fear.

Self-love can leave us feeling incomplete, but God's love equips us to be whole, assured, and genuinely fruitful in our relationships. When we return to love's divine origin, we become conduits of the love that first stirred our hearts.

In Romans 7:18, the Apostle Paul confronts us with a stark truth about human nature: in our sinful state, we inherently lack goodness. We grapple with the desire to do good, yet find ourselves incapable due to our flawed nature. Such an insight might challenge modern assertions like Christina Perri's that propose self-love as a prerequisite for loving others. The Bible offers a different perspective by suggesting that true love doesn't originate from within us.

The scriptural view is that our capacity to love authentically blossoms not from self-affirmation but from a profound love for Jesus, one that eclipses our self-focus. It's this radical love for Christ that enables us to extend grace even in the most extreme situations, such as loving someone who has caused us deep harm. This love is not a product of our own virtue but a reflection of Christ's love in us, epitomized by His sacrifice on the cross. *"Father, forgive them, for they do not know what they are doing"* (Luke 23:34), Jesus implores, setting the ultimate example of unconditional love—even in the face of great personal suffering.

Thus, while society might elevate the concept of self-love as the foundation of our ability to love others, the gospel invites us to a transformative love that begins with Jesus's love for us. Once we grasp His boundless and unwarranted love, we find a new freedom that transcends worldly standards. We become bearers of an extraordinary love that doesn't just endure but actively seeks the redemption of those who walk in darkness, much like a light piercing through the shadows.

Lucille Ball's statement can be reinterpreted through this lens as well. If faced with extreme adversity, even the presence of a terrorist, we are called not to respond with fear or hate but with a love informed by the gospel. Instead of yielding to darkness, we find strength to pray for transformation and exemplify the relentless love of Jesus. By loving Jesus with everything we have, we are indeed reborn with a new purpose: to point people toward the radical, life-changing love of Christ.

Second Motive Contrast:
SELF-DEPENDENCE VERSUS FAITH IN GOD

Webster's dictionary defines self-dependence as the ability to rely on oneself without the need for external assistance. This echoes a common adage: "If you want something done right, do it yourself." A saying I embraced wholeheartedly. Entrusting tasks to others felt like a gamble, with the results far too often falling short of my expectations. This belief led me to invest countless hours in training and instructing people, hoping this would build enough confidence in them to handle the projects I was leading.

Despite recognizing the need for collaboration to achieve growth, I found actual reliance on others challenging, especially when it came to my circle of family and friends. Missteps were met with criticism rather than encouragement, reflecting my desire for control and a misplaced sense of responsibility for ensuring perfection. I acted as the self-appointed arbiter of the 'right way'—swift to correct and criticize, believing that it underscored my capabilities and fostered trust in my judgment.

Ironically, while I prided myself on being independent and competent, my behavior was saturated with arrogance and dominance. It contradicted the humility and love I professed to uphold as a Christian. In grappling with these contradictions, I've come to acknowledge that self-dependence has its limits, and the true strength lies in our interdependence with others, facilitated by genuine trust and mutual respect.

Peter might have been one of the most self-dependent disciples we find in the Bible. He was strong-willed and outspoken. Remember Matthew 26:33 when Peter said, *"Even if all fall away on account of you, I will never fall away."* He was also very determined. Remember in John 18:10 when he took it upon himself to cut the soldier's ear off, only to have Jesus rebuke him for doing so. Peter was very sure of his abilities and often expressed them to Jesus and the other disciples.

In Matthew 4, Jesus called Peter to follow Him and Jesus told him that He was going to make Him a fisher of men. Peter even boasted about leaving everything to follow Jesus in Mark 10:28. However, Peter never fully understood what it meant to be a servant of God until Pentecost in Acts 2. We know this because, in John 21:3, self-dependent Peter went back to being a fisherman after Jesus rose from the grave. Peter was still trying to understand what it meant to walk with Jesus in such a way, that he no longer depended upon himself. He didn't quite get that God was calling Him to a new purpose for his life.

Like John the Baptist said in John 3:30 he must decrease in order for Jesus to increase. Paul understood this too, where He said in 2 Cor 5:17 that our old life has passed away and we were given a new life in Christ Jesus.

When we surrender our lives to Jesus, He reconciles us to Himself (2 Cor 5:18). Like Peter, we receive a new calling and a new dependence, no longer based on our own desires. I, too, didn't fully grasp this until later in life. My actions were driven by what I thought was best, and I felt it was my duty to make my opinions known to everyone. I was blind to the truth that once I surrendered to Jesus, my life was no longer about me. My thoughts and trust no longer mattered; it was all about what Jesus thought and how I trusted in Him.

Once I had my moment of realization, much like Peter, I began to see people differently. I started trusting Jesus with people and treating them with Christ's love. Controlling others was no longer my job. My new role was to love them to Christ. This newfound calling, dependence, and motive to trust in Jesus transformed my faith from a powerless religion into a lifestyle of change. Self-motivation turned into Jesus' promptings and guidance.

Self-dependence will never bring true freedom; it only leads to constant pain. You can rest assured that with Jesus, the opposite is true. Find the motivation to deny your self-dependence and trust Jesus with everything.

Third Motive Contrast:
SELF-WILL VERSUS SUBMISSION TO GOD

Let's consider another contrast: according to Webster's Dictionary, self-will is defined as being "stubborn or willfully adherent to one's own desire or ideas." This concept is closely related to self-dependence, but with a stronger connotation—it reflects being obstinate and, frankly, acting like a jackass. Yes, I used that word intentionally. Webster's Dictionary also defines a jackass not only as a male donkey but also as a foolish person. In my view, being foolish is deliberately doing things against God's will.

For instance, I knew lying was wrong, yet I still lied. I knew talking behind someone's back was wrong, but I still did it. I could list countless examples to illustrate this point, but the issue goes even deeper. Having self-will means taking on the role of God, ignoring the opinions and wisdom of others, particularly God's word, even when it is completely sensible. This kind of motivation is perilous.

As children of God, we must be wary of Satan's deceit, making us believe we are following God's will when we're not. I can't tell you how many times I justified my actions using God's word to make my will appear as His. Through these experiences, I've learned that any time we feel the need to justify our actions, it's a sign we're in the wrong. When we're genuinely in God's will, there's no need for justification—only trust in Him.

Saul, who later became Paul, is a prime example of someone deceived by Satan into believing that persecuting Christians was God's will. Paul was convinced that his actions were justified by scripture and saw Christians as a threat to his religion. Driven by this misguided belief, he took it upon himself to eliminate them. Had Paul taken the time to read the scriptures from God's perspective, he might have realized that his actions were not divinely sanctioned. Instead, he perceived the situation solely from his own viewpoint, leading him to conclude that Christians had to be eradicated.

Walking in our own self-will means acting solely based on what we believe is best, without truly seeing our circumstances from God's perspective. This often results in actions that, when compared to God's will, appear foolish. Paul was resolute in his mission to remove the Christian group from the earth. However, had he submitted to God, his approach would have been markedly different.

A self-willed person addresses problems in a way that makes sense to them, relying on their own judgment. In contrast, someone who submits their problems to God spends time in communion with the Father, waiting for His guidance before taking action. When a devoted follower hears from God and then proceeds to address an issue, their actions will always align with the nature of God.

What is the nature of God? We see it reflected in the fruit of the Spirit. Galatians 5:22-23 (NKJV) states: *"But the fruit of the Spirit is love, joy, peace, longsuffering, kindness, goodness, faithfulness, gentleness, self-control. Against such, there is no law."*

If Paul had been acting as a fully submitted follower of God, he would have spent time with the Father in a way that truly reflected God's character. Without surrendering his will, he would be incapable of embodying the fruit of the Spirit in any situation. Paul's zealous persecution of Christians revealed a heart filled with malice and hatred. He convinced himself that God wanted him to harm the innocent simply because they held different beliefs.

When driven by self-will, one's actions often appear foolish because they stem from the flesh rather than the Spirit. Conversely, actions motivated by submission to God will always reflect His nature. As believers, once we experience conversion, we are to set aside our own will in favor of God's will. It is not our responsibility to enforce our own desires in matters that are not of God. Instead, we are called to submit everything to the Father for His purpose and His glory.

Relying on our will places us on the throne; submitting to God places Jesus on the throne. Acting based solely on our understanding is unwise and misguided. The wisest course of action we can take is to seek to please the Father through our submission to Him. Let us be motivated to deny ourselves and submit our will to God at this very moment.

Last Motive Contrast:
SELF-SEEKING VERSUS SELF-DENIAL

In life, we are driven by two core motivations. The first is the motivation to live according to our own wants and desires. The second is the motivation to live in alignment with what God wants and desires. Operating in a self-seeking manner means acting manipulatively to ensure our own benefit. Webster defines it as "the act or practice of selfishly advancing one's own end."

When we evaluate the decisions we make each day, we need to ask ourselves: Are our choices centered around our own benefit, or are they focused on what best aligns with God's purpose and brings Him glory?

Let's consider a practical example in the context of business. Suppose we are selling a product that offers us the highest commission, but it isn't truly the best option for the client. Do we manipulate the situation to sell that product for our own gain, or do we choose to recommend what is genuinely best for the client, even though it will cost us in commission?

Moreover, when we interact with friends, do we try to persuade them to follow our desires and recommendations, or do we encourage them to seek God's will and find peace in whatever He is doing in their lives? It is essential to reflect on our motivations and strive to align them with God's desires, making decisions that honor Him rather than merely advancing our own interests.

Self-seeking individuals often find themselves restless and filled with anxiety when navigating daily life. Their minds are constantly overworking, trying to anticipate and secure what's best for themselves. They are perpetually looking ahead to tomorrow, next week, next month, or even next year in hopes of achieving their desires.

In contrast, a person motivated by self-denial is more focused on what God is doing in each moment. They embrace Jesus' teaching in Matthew 6, where He advises, "Do not worry about tomorrow, for tomorrow will take care of itself." Such individuals find peace in God's plans, content with the direction He is leading them, and humbly submit to it.

When our motives lead us to discontentment and prevent our minds from resting in Jesus, it signifies that our motives are not aligned with God's perfect will. Jesus exemplified this standard in Matthew 20:28 when He stated that He came "not to be served, but to serve." To pursue self-seeking goals contradicts the very nature of God and hinders true intimacy with the Father.

Our motivations determine whether we will experience daily victories in life. We have a choice: to position ourselves to see everything from God's perspective or to continue living based on our own feelings. Being motivated to live for Jesus alleviates many of life's headaches. While we will still face trials, we do not have to face them alone. Jesus has overcome the world, and with the help of the Holy Spirit, we too can overcome it.

Living with power from on high is possible, but it requires that our eyes are not on ourselves but fixed solely on Jesus. In the coming chapters, we will explore ways to shift our focus from ourselves to Jesus. Though this process may be painful at times, it promises to be the most rewarding and fruitful journey.

In the next chapter, we embark on a transformative journey to deepen our understanding of God's unbounded goodness. The Scripture reminds us that "the goodness of God leads us to repentance" (Romans 2:4). This divine attribute illuminates our path to genuine repentance, fostering a right perspective that anchors our trust in Him. As we delve into this truth, we can be confident that in His goodness, we find the strength to commit every aspect of our lives to His faithful care.

MOTIVES: SELF-SEEKING VS GOD SEEKING
Talking Points

1. Identify the areas in your life currently influenced by your personal motives and explain why this is the case.

2. Do your motivations align with serving Jesus? Why or why not?

3. Read 1 Peter 5:6-11 and answer the following:
   (a) What happens when we humble ourselves?

   (b) Why should we cast our cares onto Jesus first?

   (c) Who are we resisting and why?

4. Define Self-love?

5. According to Mark 12:30-31 what or who are we commanded to love?

6. Read 1 John 4:16-19 and summarize it in your own words.

7. What would be your motivation for seeking more money and recognition?

8. What drives your desire to get your way with family and friends?

9. What do you think motivates the desire for complete knowledge and power?

10. Define SELF-DEPENDENCE?

11. According to Matthew 6:33, upon whom must we be dependent on and why?

4

God Is A Good God

Isaiah 55:8 "For my thoughts are not your thoughts, neither are your ways my ways, declares the LORD."

Trusting in God amid life's trials can indeed be a profound challenge. Amid tumultuous times, it may seem as if God is distant, making our endurance diminish. It's a struggle, particularly when an internal conflict rages, tempting us to seize control for immediate relief and comprehension. We strive to be patient, to await God's guidance, yet our resolve is sorely tested when His response doesn't align with our expectations. Anxiety and frustration mount; breaths come shorter as our focus narrows to our troubles, overshadowing all else.

In this whirlwind of worry, our problems loom larger, and the rest of life's passions dim. We yearn for swift divine intervention, unwilling to bear the pain indefinitely. Our thoughts race, wrestling with doubts about God's goodness and His concern for our struggles. Hope wavers, and ironically, we find ourselves placing more faith in our ability to succeed than in the steadfastness of God's goodness.

Yet, it's in these exact moments—when hope seems faintest—that trusting in God can become a source of unshakable strength. By accepting that His timing and plans are beyond our understanding, we may find a reservoir of peace. Letting go of the need for immediate answers allows us to breathe in the faith that God is both present and loving, even when His ways are impossible to interpret. As we shift our gaze from our problems to His promises, the world regains its color, our spirit revives, and hope returns, resting on the firm foundation of divine assurance.

Acknowledging God's goodness is one thing; embodying trust in Him through our actions, especially in trying times, is another. It's easy to profess faith when life sails smoothly, but the real test unfolds during turbulence. God's wish for us in moments of distress is to adopt a posture of serene stillness and prayerful waiting.

Such trials serve as a mirror, reflecting the true nature of our faith and the depth of our reliance on Him. They compel us to introspective examination, questioning who truly holds the reins of our lives. With the affirmation that God is inherently good, we find calmness and confidence to relinquish our will, to rest peacefully in His embrace.

However, should we find anxiety and unrest upon searching deeply within our soul, it's a signal that our perception of God is distorted. A heart in turmoil is often the result of a dimmed recognition of God's goodness, a vision tainted by doubt. It is in such moments that we must guard against the creeping shadow of disbelief, ensuring it does not obscure our sense of His profound goodness. When we adjust our sight to the unalterable truth that God is GOOD, it's then we become impenetrable to the adversary's attempts to veil the reality of His unwavering kindness.

Garden of Eden

As a Pastor to both the faithful and seekers alike, I am often presented with a probing question about the divine character and the perplexities of life. A question that frequently arises is this: " If God is good, why does He allow bad things to happen to good people?" Addressing this question is no small task, and the forthcoming discussion will be an effort to answer this question. But let's ground our dialogue in a foundational truth: embracing this life and overcoming its challenges through surrender necessitates an unshakable belief in God's inherent goodness.

The crux of many people's hesitancy to place unwavering trust in Jesus stems from the deceptions sown by Satan, which distorts the true nature of God. These falsehoods fabricate an image of a harsh, punitive God, preoccupied with retribution—a stark contrast to the reality of God's character. To navigate these misconceptions, let us explore the essence of divine goodness and love, affirming the truth of Psalms 136:1: "Give thanks to the LORD, for He is good, for His lovingkindness is everlasting."

Misunderstandings about God's holiness have unfortunately led to a tarnished reputation, viewed by some as stern and vindictive, exacting death as a penalty for non-conformity. This wrong perception neglects the depth of God's love and the purpose behind His precepts. The belief that God is on a relentless quest to punish sinners is one of Satan's most cunning lies. In the following paragraphs, I aim to illuminate the reality of God's goodness and the profound scope of His love, which is not hindered by our shortcomings.

> *John 8:44 says "You are of your father the devil, and you want to do the desires of your father He was a murderer from the beginning, and does not stand in the truth because there is no truth in him whenever he speaks a lie, he speaks from his own nature, for he is a liar and the father of lies."*

Satan often tries to make us believe that God is against us and constantly angry at us for our mistakes. However, as mentioned above, this is far from the truth. We must actively replace these falsehoods with the truth of God's unwavering goodness. Many of us have struggled in our Christian walk because we've unknowingly accepted these deceitful notions. We've come to think that God is against us, but this could not be further from reality. This chapter aims to provide an overview of the Bible, illustrating why God is inherently good and deserving of our complete trust. My goal is to help us internalize God's truth, ensuring that Satan's lies no longer have any power over us by making us doubt God's goodness.

To fully grasp the goodness of God, we need to start at the very beginning, where it is stated that God created the heavens and the earth (Genesis 1:1). Often, our perception of God is not entirely accurate. By reflecting on this foundational point, we can revisit familiar concepts and potentially gain a fresh perspective. Even for those already seeing things this way, it serves as a valuable review and a moment for glorifying God.

I'm not a scientist, nor do I intend to present myself as one. I am simply someone who believes that God created the heavens and the earth. There are many experts who can delve into this topic with far greater scientific rigor. My approach is straightforward and from the heart. Like many, I have pondered whether life happened by chance or through a creator. For me, the answer is clear: design implies a designer, and creation implies a creator.

I believe that the assertion against divine creation is one of the deceptions used to lead people away from belief in God. Convincing you either way is beyond my purview. However, I believe in God's goodness because, as Genesis 1:31 (NKJV) states, "Then God saw everything that He had made, and indeed it was very good."

God made man to have fellowship with Him. He gave them everything created, except for the Tree of Knowledge. *Gen 2:17 NKJV "But of the tree of the knowledge of good and evil you shall not eat, for in the day that you eat of it you shall surely die."* God did not create man to be a robot for him but to be a man who can think and make choices. That is a good

God. He also made a planet that was perfect in every way without flaws. A place where man can spend all eternity in fellowship with God. That is why man lived so long back in the Old Testament days. Remember in Gen 5:27, it says Methuselah lived 969 years, Adam 930 years in Gen 5:4, and Noah 950 years, etc. Remember that everything that God does is perfect and Holy. There is nothing God can do that is bad but only good and not just good but perfect. He made the earth perfect and it's where He desired man to live with Him in perfect fellowship forever- that is until man's sin changed that.

In Genesis 2:21-23, it is said that God created woman for man, giving her the name Eve, as Adam's helper. The foresight and provision God demonstrated by creating a helpmate for Adam is, for me, clear evidence of His goodness. Personally, I can't imagine where I'd be without my wife; she completes me in countless ways. Together, Adam and Eve enjoyed perfect fellowship with God in His creation. Everything was in harmony until the day Satan deceived Eve (Genesis 3:6).

This brings up an important question: Why did God allow Satan into His perfect garden with Adam and Eve? If He is a good God, why didn't He protect them from Satan's deception? This is a fair question, which leads to another important one: Why wouldn't God give us the option to choose His goodness or another way?

True love involves choice. If all we knew was good and nothing bad, would that really be genuine love? Having the freedom to choose allows us the liberty to act according to our beliefs and feelings. Without choice, our actions would be forced, potentially leading to resentment and rebellion. Thus, the presence of choice is fundamental to the concept of true love and freedom.

The remarkable thing is that God's goodness extends even to giving us choices, while also guiding us toward what is best. In Genesis 3:3, God warned Adam of the consequences of a particular choice. Similarly, He warns us today that certain paths lead to death and destruction. Out of His goodness, He lays everything out clearly for us to make informed decisions.

God is sovereign and does as He pleases (Psalm 115:3). Regardless of our perceptions, He acts in ways that are ultimately best for us. In the case of Adam and Eve, He allowed them the freedom to choose, demonstrating His care and goodness. Unfortunately, they made the wrong choice, resulting in God cursing the ground for their sake.

> *Genesis 3:22 says NKJV "Then the LORD God said, Behold, the man has become like one of us, to know good and evil. And now, lest he put out his hand and take also of the tree of life, and eat, and live forever."*

This act of disobedience fundamentally altered mankind from what God originally intended. The moment Adam chose to go against God's perfect will, the environment in which he lived changed dramatically. As a result, God had to send him out of the perfect garden, into a life of hardship and pain.

From that point on, God's role in Adam's life shifted. He became Adam's comforter and guide, though not without the accompanying pain that sin would bring. This new reality marked the beginning of a life where God's comfort and guidance were essential amidst the consequences of disobedience.

> Theologian Charles Ellicott explained this best when he said "All those qualities which constitute man's likeness to God— free-will, self-dependence, the exercise of reason and of choice —had been developed by the fall, and Adam was now a very different being from what he had been in the days of his simple innocence. Adam had exercised the power of marring God's work, and if an unending physical life were added to the gift of

free will now in revolt against God, his condition and that of mankind would become most miserable. Man is still to attain to immortality, but it must now be through struggle, sorrow, penitence, faith, and death. Hence a paradise is no fit home for him. The Divine mercy, therefore, commands Adam to quit it, in order that he may live under conditions better suited for his moral and spiritual good."[vi]

God is holy (1 Peter 1:16), meaning He is perfect. Words alone cannot fully capture the depth of what this means. As Isaiah 55:8 tells us, "For my thoughts are not your thoughts, neither are your ways my ways, declares the LORD." Whatever we might think we know, God knows infinitely more. It is foolish to believe we can compare our understanding to His. Psalm 99:5 reminds us to "Exalt the LORD our God and worship at His footstool; holy is He."

It's important to remember that before Adam's fall, he enjoyed perfect fellowship with God in all His holiness. Paradise, as Adam experienced it, was complete. It was a place of comfort, joy, and freedom from fear or want. Adam's delight was in the Lord and he needed nothing else but God's presence. However, after sin entered the world, paradise was lost, and with it came the hardships and struggles that we all face today.

The world changed drastically with Adam's fall. Sin began to dominate the human experience, corrupting and destroying what was once perfect. Death entered this world that a good God had originally created without flaw. As a result, humanity is now in a constant search for the lost paradise and the perfection that God had intended from the beginning.

Our quest for relief from pain is, at its heart, a longing for the Garden—a place free from worry and fear. Jesus, in His grace, offers to restore us to that state. Without Him, we are left with only the brokenness of this fallen world. We will explore this in greater detail later, but for now, understand that through Jesus, hope is restored, and God's goodness is revealed.

Without Jesus, humanity is driven by personal desires and subjective notions of what is best. In a world marred by sin, people attempt to create their own sense of purpose, often leading to a life disconnected from God. As a result, individuals inflict harm on others and experience their own pain. In seeking solace from this suffering, many turn to harmful habits that further blind them to the goodness of God.

This downward spiral perpetuates a cycle of destruction, making the prospect of finding true goodness seem unattainable without divine intervention. Satan eagerly offers distractions that lead people away from God, and in their refusal to recognize God's goodness, they readily accept these counterfeit comforts. Consequently, their lives become filled with tumultuous highs and lows, as darkness increasingly over-shadows the light.

The Bible says that Satan is the god of this world and his whole purpose of existence is to deceive people from seeing that God is good.

> *2 Cor 4:4 NLT "Satan, who is the god of this world, has blinded the minds of those who don't believe. They are unable to see the glorious light of the Good News. They don't understand this message about the glory of Christ, who is the exact likeness of God."*

The fall of Adam, and by extension to us, had made man believe that he is his own god because he can now determine the difference between good and evil. *(Gen 2:17)* Man now determines what he deems is best and controls his life the way he thinks he should go. Man has always had a choice to trust God or to trust in himself. Unfortunately, today most of the world now trusts in themselves and their own beliefs.

The fall of Adam led humanity to believe that we are our own gods, determining right and wrong for ourselves (Genesis 2:17). This newfound autonomy has driven people to make their own judgments and control their lives as they see fit. Throughout history, mankind has faced the choice to trust in God or in themselves. Unfortunately, today, many choose to rely on their own understanding and beliefs.

With this background on sin and God's inherent goodness, let's revisit the initial question: If God is good, why does He allow bad things to happen to good people? Based on our discussion, it's clear that a good God did not cause sin to befall a good person. Instead, humans have free will to choose righteousness according to God or sin according to Satan. Thus, does a good God desire sin to happen to a good person? Absolutely not! God despises sin. As Psalm 97:10 states, "Let those who love the LORD hate evil." Sin brings destruction, never goodness.

Anything the world offers outside of Christ will never lead to true goodness. Sin is always destructive, while God is perpetually good and gracious. Even though mankind willfully chose sin over God, can good still emerge from bad situations? Yes! In Romans 8:28, it is written, *"All things work together for good to those who love God, to those who are called according to His purpose."*

To conclude this section: God is inherently good, while sin is inherently bad. He grants humanity the free will to choose between trusting Him and doing good or engaging in sin and causing harm. In the next section, we will see how Jesus is the greatest gift a good God could ever bestow upon mankind. We'll tackle more challenging questions and uncover how God has consistently loved and pursued humanity throughout history.

Jesus - the best gift a good God
could have ever given mankind

To begin this section, let's delve deeper into the holiness of God, a concept we touched on earlier. A common question I encounter is, "If God is good, why did He allow the killing of so many people in the Old Testament when the Israelites were entering the Promised Land?

Because God is good, He chose a people to be set apart in a sinful world, demonstrating His goodness to all humanity. By selecting the Israelites, God intended to show the world how to live in communion with a perfect and holy God. He provided them with specific instructions on how to act in all aspects of life and taught them to worship Him in a manner that He, being perfect, could accept.

On a side note, I write about the rejection of the world and God's choice of Israel extensively in my book "Three Grand Rebellions." I highly recommend reading it to better understand the historical context and gain new insights into God's goodness.

However, despite humanity's flaws, God's holiness did not lead Him to abandon us. Instead, He chose to pursue us and shower His grace upon us. By setting apart the Israelites, God aimed to reveal His goodness and provide a model for living in a relationship with Him.

The land that God gave to Israel was inhabited by nations that did not fear Him, nor were they holy. Because God is holy, He needed to remove anything that could lead His chosen people astray. While this might be difficult to comprehend, it's important to remember that we are not God, and our ways are not His ways. Who are we to question why God does what He does? What we do know is that He is good and desires everyone to come to the knowledge of His truth (1 Timothy 2:4).

God needed to sanctify the Israelites, setting them apart from the world. Anything unholy had to be removed from among them and within them. To ensure the Israelites were distinct, God could not allow the influence of the evil nations around them. He set them apart in such a way that the whole world could one day be saved through their lineage.

God is holy and cannot tolerate sin. To set His people apart, He needed to cleanse the land of all evil so that He could be properly glorified. Once this was accomplished, God could fulfill the covenants He made with Israel. These covenants are crucial because they pave the way for the forgiveness of our sins, showing that God is truly good. Let me explain further.

God's first covenant was given to Abraham long before the Israelites entered the Promised Land. He promised Abraham that his descendants would be as numerous as the stars in the sky (Genesis 26:4). This covenant is significant because it extends the opportunity for salvation to the Gentiles (non-Jewish descendants). I'll discuss this in more context later, but for now, know that this covenant is incredibly good news.

The second covenant God made with Israel is known as the Mosaic Covenant. God gave Moses His divine law in the form of the Ten Commandments on Mount Sinai.

> "This covenant would serve to set the nation of Israel apart from all other nations as God's chosen people and was as equally binding as the unconditional covenant that God made with Abraham because it is also a blood covenant. The Mosaic Covenant is a significant covenant in both God's redemptive history and in the history of the nation of Israel through whom God would sovereignly choose to bless the world with His written Word and the Living Word, Jesus Christ. The Mosaic Covenant was centered around God giving His divine law to Moses on Mount Sinai." (Exodus 31:18)[vii]

This covenant is good news because without God giving Moses the law, we would never know the difference between what is right and what is wrong. More importantly without this covenant, we would never see how unholy we actually are and how desperate we are for a Savior. Because God is good, He gave us His law and Jesus to save us from His Holy law. I will explain more of this a little later as well.

The final covenant we will discuss is the one God made with David, found in 2 Samuel 7. In this covenant, God promised David and Israel that the Messiah—Jesus—would come from David's lineage and the tribe of Judah. This covenant points directly to the central theme of this chapter: God's goodness in providing a Savior for us.

Jesus is our lifeline, given by God to save us from our sins. Without Him, we would remain hopeless sinners with no escape from sin. It was through God's choice of Israel to bring forth Jesus that we came to understand our need for a Savior. Without this, we would have remained blinded by Satan, devoid of hope for eternity.

Paul explains this phenomenon best in *Romans 5:12-21 NKJV*

> *12 Therefore, just as through one man sin entered the world, and death through sin, and thus death spread to all men, because all sinned— 13 (For until the law sin was in the world, but sin is not imputed when there is no law. 14 Nevertheless death reigned from Adam to Moses, even over those who had not sinned according to the likeness of the transgression of Adam, who is a type of Him who was to come. 15 But the free gift is not like the offense. For if by the one man's offense many died, much more the grace of God and the gift by the grace of the one Man, Jesus Christ, abounded to many. 16 And the gift is not like that which came through the one who sinned. For the judgment which came from one offense resulted in condemnation, but the free gift which came from many offenses resulted in justification. 17 For if by the one man's offense death*

reigned through the one, much more those who receive abundance of grace and of the gift of righteousness will reign in life through the One, Jesus Christ.

[18] Therefore, as through one man's offense judgment came to all men, resulting in condemnation, even so through one Man's righteous act the free gift came to all men, resulting in justification of life. [19] For as by one man's disobedience many were made sinners, so also by one Man's obedience many will be made righteous.[20] Moreover the law entered that the offense might abound. But where sin abounded, grace abounded much more, [21] so that as sin reigned in death, even so grace might reign through righteousness to eternal life through Jesus Christ our Lord.

God not only gives us Jesus to save us from our sins, but He also offers us the hope of eternal life with Him—just as He intended from the very beginning. Through Jesus, we are granted access to the garden once more, in Him we are given the keys to the Kingdom per se. Sin once separated us from peace with God, but with Jesus, we have found the answer the world has always been searching for eternal peace, even if they didn't realize it.

Jesus becomes our refuge in times of trouble, our beacon of hope in times of despair, our source of comfort in times of suffering, and our provider in times of need. Through Him, we can now enjoy the fellowship with God that Adam experienced in the beginning. Even though this world is deteriorating and will ultimately come to an end, Jesus provides us with the hope of a new heaven and a new earth (Revelation 21).

Moreover, He fills our current lives with unspeakable joy. As 1 Peter 1:8 (ESV) says, "Though you have not seen him, you love him. Though you do not now see him, you believe in him and rejoice with joy that is inexpressible and filled with glory."

The covenants in the Old Testament were based on the Law. I don't know about you but I have tried to walk by the law, only to realize that I always fall short.

> Galatians 3:13-14 NKJV says "Christ has redeemed us from the curse of the law, having become a curse for us (for it is written, Cursed is everyone who hangs on a tree.) That the blessing of Abraham might come upon the Gentiles in Christ Jesus, that we might receive the promise of the Spirit through faith."

Remember when I mentioned I would revisit the covenant with Abraham? Here it is. God's goodness is evident in His grace and provision, which allow us to partake in Abraham's covenant through our faith in Jesus. The new covenant that God established through Jesus is one of grace, but without the foundation of Abraham's covenant, we wouldn't have access to it.

The Apostle Paul presents a profound insight into the nature of faith and righteousness through the legacy of Abraham in Romans 4:1-3 and 16-17.

He poses a reflective question about what Abraham, the patriarch, had gained according to the flesh. Paul clarifies that if Abraham's righteousness had been based on his deeds, he would have reason to boast—but not before God. Instead, Paul cites the Scripture, which resonates with a timeless truth: "Abraham believed God, and it was credited to him as righteousness."

Emphasizing the importance of faith, Paul teaches that righteousness comes by faith in order to align with grace, ensuring that God's promise extends to all Abraham's descendants—not only to those adhering to the Law but also to those sharing the faith of Abraham. Paul quotes the promise made to Abraham, "A father of many nations have I made you," which illuminates Abraham's role in God's plan, showing that

God brings life from the dead and summons into existence that which did not exist before.

This theme of faith extending beyond lineage is further explored by Paul in Romans 9:6-8, where he points out that not all physical descendants of Israel are of true Israel. Nor does being a biological descendant of Abraham automatically equate to being a child of God. Rather, it is the children of the promise—those who inherit Abraham's faith—who are the true descendants.

The paradigm set by Abraham's faith transcends mere ancestry and underscores that it is not through human works or lineage that we are reconciled with God, but through faith. This foundational truth becomes the bedrock for the proclamation of the Gospel to every corner of the earth, affirming that salvation is offered first to the Jew and also to the gentile.

This inclusive promise is the reason we are all invited to share in the Good News, joining the family of faith that dates back to the covenant with Abraham. Through faith, we are grafted into this sprawling, diverse family—a family not confined by ethnic or cultural barriers, but one that is bound together by belief in the promises of God. Because of this promise, Paul writes *"For by grace you have been saved through faith, and that not of yourselves, it is the gift of God. Not of works, lest anyone should boast."* Ephesians 2:8 NKJV

Recap: Divine Goodness and Human Choice

We have learned that God is inherently good and desires a relationship with humanity. Although man chose to sin, through Jesus, we are granted the choice to be saved from that sin or to continue living in it, leading to eternal separation from God. God is holy and perfect, and questioning His ways is both imprudent and unwise. His grace, accessed through faith, is what saves us; it's our choice to believe this truth or not.

The Journey of Faith: Choosing Jesus

We have two paths: continuing in sin, which results in a hopeless future, or embracing Jesus and being freed from sin's bondage. As a simple man, I choose Jesus and the hope He offers. I find joy and rest in Him, rather than living in misery and attempting to control my destiny, which is both exhausting and futile.

Trials as Pathways to Closeness with God

Although trials come, they do not negate God's goodness. Instead, trials are opportunities for us to draw closer to Him. In every situation, we can find His goodness, for God is good all the time.

In later chapters, we will delve deeper into the trials we face and how we can view them from God's perspective. Understanding the purposes of trials from God's perspective will change everything. This is where our spiritual growth begins to take shape. In the next chapter, we will explore why cultivating a deeper, more intimate relationship with Jesus is essential for understanding how to navigate and overcome life's trials.

GOD IS A GOOD GOD
Talking Points

1. Read Isaiah 55:8. What does this verse mean to you?

2. Have you ever struggled to believe in God's goodness during difficult times in your life? Share your experience.

3. Why do you think it's so challenging to "be still" and trust God when your life challenges seem to make no sense?

4. Read 2 Corinthians 4:3-4 and answer the following: What scriptural evidence supports the claim that Satan acts as the 'god of this world'?

5. Why did God separate the Israelites from other nations, and how did He accomplish this?

6. How can sin cloud your perception of God's goodness? Explain

7. How does Jesus save us from the Law, according to Galatians 3:13-14?

8. What does it mean to you to "be holy"?

9. Describe what it means to you to have access through Jesus to the Garden of Eden once again.

10. What does it mean to you that God is good and that He is the answer in our trials?

5

Deepening Your Walk with Christ

Jesus said to him, "Have you believed because you have seen me? Blessed are those who have not seen and yet have believed." John 20:29 ESV

In our previous chapter, we embarked on an enlightening journey that revealed the unwavering goodness of God, standing in stark contrast to the sickness of sin that leads to death. It becomes clear that God's nature is pure and loving, with His arms stretched wide, yearning for each one of us to relish in everlasting peace by His side. With God on our side, His boundless grace grants us the gift of salvation through His Son, Jesus Christ.

As John 3:16 affirms, it's through Jesus that this sublime connection with God becomes possible. Apart from Jesus, the barrier of our sins severs our access to the Father. Yet, in embracing Him, we are welcomed into an intimate fellowship with God. Hebrews 4:16 says *"We can now approach God's throne room with boldness."*

Jesus' mission on Earth was one of cosmic rescue: to redeem us from the entanglements of sin and the decay of this world. Through His sacrifice, He instills a beacon of hope within us, illuminating a path forward to a future filled with promise.

The Scriptures offer a captivating vision: One of our greatest hopes in Jesus is the promise that one day we will dwell with Him on a new Earth, where eternity unfolds before us in endless glory (Revelation 21). This future promise brims with a hope that is not only distant but also immediate and powerful—it inspires us to live holy lives today, guided by the teachings of Jesus (1 Peter 1:16).

In Jesus, we know our future is guaranteed, but there is a lot of confusion about how we can live a holy life in Jesus now. This chapter is intended to provide us with this wisdom and teach us how to navigate life's challenges by following Jesus' example.

Understanding and following His path are key to finding joy and resilience in the face of life's inevitable trials. In doing so, we don't just brace ourselves against hardship but also arm ourselves with the strength to resist the lures of a flawed and tempting world.

Our sins, along with the sins of the world, inevitably bring us pain and disrupt our holy living. However, by knowing Jesus intimately and studying His word, we can find guidance to avoid the temptations of sin. It's important to remember that in Jesus, there is no condemnation for those who belong to Him (Romans 8:1). While Satan may remind us of our sins to condemn us, Jesus constantly reminds us of His love and forgiveness.

Paul expresses this well in Philippians 1:21, where he says, *"For to me, to live is Christ and to die is gain."* Paul eagerly anticipated eternal life with Jesus, yet also recognized the importance of living according to Jesus' teachings while on earth. Jesus provides clear instructions for this way of living in Matthew 22:37, where He commands us to *"Love the Lord your God with all your heart and with all your soul and with all your mind,"* and in verse 22:39, to *"Love your neighbor as yourself."*

Reading the Bible daily is crucial to learning how to live as Jesus did. Without daily engagement with the Scriptures, developing a deep, personal relationship with Jesus becomes challenging. It's essential to know Jesus personally, and through diligent study of His word along with ample quiet time, we can learn to understand who He is and how profoundly He loves us.

The title of this book, "Conquer Through Surrender," draws from Romans 8:37, which states that through Jesus, who loves us, we are more than conquerors in all things. This concept emphasizes that without surrendering our lives to Jesus, true conquest is unattainable. By "conquer," I refer to living in the Spirit, as opposed to a life lived by the world's standards in the flesh. I will delve deeper into this distinction in the forthcoming chapters.

Many of us are familiar with Jesus. We can quote Bible verses and may have occasionally shared our faith with others. I can relate to being a "fan" of Jesus—someone who admires and knows about Him. However, being a true "follower" of Jesus is an entirely different journey, one that took me a significant part of my life to understand and embark upon. This crucial difference is thoroughly explored in Kyle Idleman's book, "Not a Fan,"[viii] which I highly recommend. Idleman challenges his readers to examine whether they are merely fans of Jesus or genuine followers, a question that is pivotal for our spiritual growth.

To illustrate his point, Kyle Idleman used a memorable example in chapter 3 of his book. He described a poster and a picture he had on his wall as a kid: the poster was of the famous basketball player, Michael Jordan, and the picture was of Jesus. Kyle shared that he was a fan of both; he knew their statistics well and could tell you everything about them. However, he realized he was not a true follower of either.

Kyle didn't know Michael Jordan personally. He couldn't tell you what Michael was like during his downtime or what he thought about. If he were a genuine follower, he would have known intimate details about Michael—how he reacted when he was upset, or what his favorite food was when he was happy. A true follower knows the intimate nuances of someone's life, not just their public achievements.

The same principle applied to Jesus. Kyle could recite facts about Jesus, knew His deeds, and could quote His words. Yet, he admitted he didn't know Jesus intimately. Kyle's book, along with this one, is designed to guide followers of Jesus into a deeper, more intimate relationship with Him. They aim to help people see Jesus in every aspect of their lives, moving beyond mere knowledge to a genuine, personal connection. As Kyle suggests, we are called to become true followers of Jesus, not just fans.

Reflecting on my early childhood, I remember a profound experience when I was about six or seven that I seldom speak of. It revolves around an incident that strengthened my belief in the spiritual realm interwoven within our own—a lesson in the very real presence of demonic forces.

This chapter of my life began with a hidden Playboy magazine in my father's bathroom. Unbeknownst to us at the time, this book acted as a conduit for an evil spirit into our home. It's partly because of the sensitive nature of this origin that I rarely recount this true story.

The presence of this demonic entity became alarmingly evident to my grandfather, affectionately known as Papa Eric. One night, as he slept in the living room, he was confronted with the chilling image of a terrifying face. Twice this happened, and twice his reaction was the same: With firm conviction, he would command the spirit to depart in Jesus' name—and it obeyed, albeit leaving behind a trail of fear.

The link between the magazine and the unwelcome visitor was unveiled during a family prayer meeting—an assembly of family and friends united in a single purpose to cleanse our house. It was during this spiritual gathering that the Holy Spirit stirred my father to realize the root cause of our problem. Taking decisive action, we took the magazine and incinerated it on the grill in our backyard, a symbolic act of purification and a testament to our faith in the face of fear.

As I recount these memories, I recognize that some may feel inclined to not believe me. Yet, what I'm about to share stems from genuine occurrences, validated by numerous eyewitnesses. I intend to relay events as I recall them, acknowledging that debating these experiences is unlikely to be productive.

The fear that gripped me in the aftermath was unparalleled. My young life was consumed by sheer terror; I could not sleep, eat, or even attend to the simplest personal tasks on my own. I was utterly paralyzed by fear.

Amidst the burning of the magazine, an incident occurred that further cemented my alarm. As the pages turned to ash on the grill, the demon's image emerged from the embers, a sight that didn't escape the eyes of the onlookers gathered around. My father, Papa Eric, and I acted quickly. Using a brown paper grocery bag, we collected the ashes. After securing the top, my father and I carried it down the street to an open sewer. It was a rainy night, and the currents flowed eagerly into the sewer, providing the perfect moment to dispose of the ashes. We tossed the sealed bag into the gushing waters, only to witness a black cloud of ash erupted from the drain moments later. Such an occurrence defied explanation, especially in the rainy weather with a sealed bag. This inexplicable phenomenon led me to fear the return of the demon even more.

The persistent terror was debilitating, lasting weeks on end. Recognizing my distress, my mother decided to take action. Believing in the necessity of prayer from the elders at our church, the pastor and elders anointed me with oil as described in James 5:14-15, seeking divine healing. What happened next was beyond my mother's expectations—and mine. A profound healing was on the horizon, about to unfold in ways that we could not have anticipated. The change it brought was nothing short of miraculous.

The night I was sleeping on the floor of my bedroom, an unusual arrangement thanks to my sister and grandmother occupying the two beds available—a tale in itself that could easily fill another book with its details. But let's get back to the heart of this story.

Adjacent to my makeshift sleeping quarters, my baby brother battled the Hong Kong Flu, his breathing composed of ghastly noises that, to my frightened mind, mimicked the sinister whispers of a demon. The nightfall did not bring rest but amplified every fear, for the house came alive with creaks and groans, a chorus of eerie sounds that seemed to play a sinister symphony.

Amidst the backdrop of these unsettling noises, the situation grew more dire as my sister and grandmother began to snore, a soundtrack that to my ears spelled imminent doom. I lay there enveloped in dread, convinced that the demon, lured by the night's noise, had come for a dreadful visitation.

Clutching to the teachings my Mom and Papa Eric had instilled in me, I focused on the potent name of Jesus, believing in its power to repel darkness. With each repetition of "In the Name of Jesus, flee," I transitioned from a silent mantra to a vocal proclamation, summoning courage from the depths of my soul.

Amidst this fervent watch, a knock sounded at my window, sharp and unexpected. The fear that seized me was automatic, a fright so intense I nearly leaped from my skin. This moment tested every ounce of my resolve, every snippet of faith I held dear, and brought me face to face with the night's deepest shadows.

I glanced over at my window and noticed that my blinds, which had been closed earlier, were now open. The backyard was bathed in an ethereal white light, unlike anything I had ever seen before, or since. Hovering above the shrubs was Jesus, His arms and hands outstretched, and His feet together as if pierced by a nail. An indescribable peace washed over me, accompanied by an overwhelming sense of love emanating from Him, though He spoke not a word aloud. The scars on His hands and feet were visible to me, and then He communicated directly to my spirit: "Go to sleep, Petee, go to sleep, for I Am with you." Petee is the nickname my parents call me, as my dad's name is also Pete.

In my excitement, I leaped onto my grandma's bed to wake her so she could witness Jesus too. Startled at first, she got up just in time to see Jesus ascending into heaven. Filled with uncontainable joy, I recounted the incredible experience to her and then to the rest of the household. Despite all my excitement, part of me still struggled with lingering fears the next day.

The following night, as I went to bed, the same fear crept back. Wide awake and panicked, I again heard a familiar knock on the window. Once again, the blinds were open, and the backyard was illuminated with that same brilliant white light. This time, however, it was a hand waving at me. Whether it was Jesus' hand or not, the message to my spirit was unmistakable and comforting: "Go to sleep, Petee, go to sleep, for I Am with you."

From that night forward, all fear left me, and my mom was amazed at the transformation. She describes it as nothing short of miraculous. I share this story to illustrate that although I saw Jesus and believed in His reality, for a long time I only knew Him superficially. I was a fan, well-acquainted with His "statistics," but not a true follower. For much of my life, I believed in Jesus but never fully trusted Him.

John 20:29 ESV Jesus said to him, "Have you believed because you have seen me? Blessed are those who have not seen and yet have believed."

I have often heard people say that if they could only see Jesus with their own eyes, they would believe in Him. While my own belief stemmed from physically seeing Him, this experience alone did not make me a true follower. Seeing Jesus can affirm His existence, but it doesn't necessarily lead to genuine discipleship.

Satan has effectively clouded the minds of believers, causing confusion about what and why they believe. It is challenging to adopt Jesus' perspective without relinquishing control of our own lives. As the author and finisher of our faith (Heb 12:2), God orchestrates everything. Through my experience, God taught me to be strong and courageous, always reminding me of His constant presence. He knew I would need this strength to endure the trials and tribulations I have faced.

Joshua 1:9 NLT says "Be strong and courageous! Do not be afraid or discouraged. For the Lord your God is with you wherever you go."

As a 7-year-old boy, I did not fully grasp the reality that Jesus was always with me. It wasn't until later in life that I truly comprehended this truth. My eyes were opened to His goodness as I began to trust Him more and lay down my own life. Matthew 16:25 (ESV) says, *"For whoever would save his life will lose it, but whoever loses his life for my sake will find it."* When I realized that Jesus is for me, my faith began to grow. I started to let go of what I thought was best for me and embraced what Jesus knew was best for my life.

Shallow End Living and Deep end Living

We've all heard the saying that we need to move from the shallow end to the deep end. The shallow end represents our comfort zone, where we can control the outcome of any situation. In contrast, the deep end is where we step out of our comfort zone, with no shore to cling to or foundation to stand on. It's unknown territory, and it's there that we learn to rely solely on Jesus. Walking in the shallow end means being a Christian who attends church and maybe even Bible studies but never truly rests in God during challenging times. Walking in the deep end with Jesus means that we live fully for Him, resting in His presence no matter the circumstances. Deep-end living involves moving at God's pace and surrendering to His will. In contrast, shallow-end living involves keeping one foot in the world (control) and one foot with Jesus.

Shallow End Living

A shallow-end Christian is afraid to let go of their perceived peace of mind, fearing the unknown and lack of control. They seek peace but struggle to find it because they are always trying to figure out what comes next. They feel the need to have the final say or be part of the decision-making process. This type of Christianity justifies its stance with God's word without truly knowing if it's God's word for their life.

In later chapters, we will look deeper into these concepts, but the main point is that without deep-end living, we can never fully know Jesus.

At one point, I considered myself a shallow-end Christian, constantly yearning for a deep relationship with Jesus but never quite knowing how to achieve it. I vividly remember a conversation many years ago with my friend Pastor Rick that left a lasting impression on me. He raised both of his hands in front of him, interlocking his fingers, and said, "I look to see what Jesus is doing, and when He is at work, everything comes together," while demonstrating by opening and closing his hands. What he was conveying was for us, as followers of Jesus, to observe what the Father is doing and then act upon it.

As a shallow-end Christian trying to control my life, I was never able to clearly see what God was doing. Consequently, I couldn't experience a deep, intimate, and real relationship with Jesus. During the times I needed Him the most, I felt distant and shallow. Maybe you can relate.

It was only when I finally let go of my life that I began to truly deepen my relationship with Jesus. At that point, I could finally understand what He was saying and asking of me. But what does it mean to let go of your life? For me, it meant surrendering my dreams, my job, my family, my wants, my desires, and my wealth. It meant deciding not to fight circumstances anymore but to lay them at the foot of the cross. I made a conscious decision in my mind to fully surrender my will to Him, which then allowed Him to instigate the painful but necessary changes within me.

Deep End Living

Deep-end living brings us to the realization that Jesus is our sole guide to living in a way that pleases the Father. We have the Bible, especially the Gospels, to study and learn from how Jesus lived His life and depended on His Father. However, if we do not relinquish our control and learn to be still before Him, studying His life will remain mere knowledge and never transform into reality.

Deep-end living opens our eyes to the truth that Jesus never did anything without first seeing His Father do it. Jesus lived solely to please the Father. In John 14:26, Jesus promises that His Father will send the Holy Spirit to us as an advocate to teach us everything and to remind us of all that Jesus has taught. One of the primary roles of the Holy Spirit is to remind us of everything Jesus has told us in His gospel. God, in His goodness, desires for us to achieve victory in life, but this victory comes only through Jesus and the help of the Holy Spirit.

What does victory look like? To God, victory is a person transformed by the renewing of their mind (Romans 12:2). Transformed into what? Into the image of Jesus (Romans 8:29). Remember from our last chapter that God is holy and perfect, and it is sin that is bad, not God. When we walk through this world without following Jesus' lead and without relying on the Holy Spirit for guidance, we fall short of holiness. Our image will increasingly resemble the god of this world, Satan, and our lifestyle will reflect that divergence.

> *1 John 5:19 "We know that we are from God, and the whole world lies in the power of the evil one."*

God is a good God! He desires perfection for us—not a perfection that condemns, but one that embodies His goodness. Jesus lived a perfect life on this earth, thriving in every moment and using His gifts for God's glory. He was able to do this because He continuously sought the Father. When we've given our lives over to Jesus, we come under His control, allowing His perfection to reign in us.

The Father may allow challenging circumstances in our lives to teach us to shift our focus from the situation to His Son. In His goodness, the Father gives us the Holy Spirit to help us understand everything that Jesus has taught. This process can be painful and longer than we might desire, but over time and with the Holy Spirit's help, we begin to look more and more like Jesus.

Ask yourself these questions: Do you desire to love like Jesus loved? Do you want to have peace amid storms? Do you long for the power to move mountains? Do you aspire to thrive in every moment given by the Father? There are countless questions like these, and if your answer is 'Yes' to any of them, you'll find that the only answer is Jesus.

Deep-end Christians understand the process required to be molded and shaped to look like Jesus. They embrace it and, as a result, experience the fullness of God's plan for their lives. Shallow-end Christians, on the other hand, resist this process and, therefore, never fully experience everything that God has planned for their lives.

Deep-end Christians naturally experience God's masterpiece for themselves and, over time, see it more clearly. Shallow-end Christians catch only glimpses of this beauty and always find themselves longing for more.

God knew that because of our sins, we couldn't save ourselves. So, He sent His only Son to live a perfect life and satisfy His holy requirements on our behalf. Jesus came to earth as both fully man and fully God, experiencing everything we do, including pain. He is our perfect example of how to live a victorious life through purposeful surrender, just as the Father originally intended.

Without God sending Jesus to save us from our sins, we could never be one with the Father as Jesus was (John 17:21). In this world, we will face challenging circumstances and injustices that leave us needing direction. When we turn to the world, it offers mere pain relievers and excuses that temporarily mask our problems. However, when we turn to Jesus, He addresses our problems from the perspective of Truth.

To help us understand that He can be trusted, Jesus experienced the same pain and suffering on this earth that we do. He modeled the way we should respond in all situations. By knowing that Jesus felt what we feel, we can relate to Him better with our limited understanding. When we examine and study the life of Jesus, focusing on how He dealt with circumstances, we learn how the Father desires for us to walk.

God's love was so immense that by sending Jesus, He provided the ultimate truth that everyone is searching for (John 14:6). What is this truth? It is the understanding that we were created to bring glory to God. Every person on this planet seeks purpose in their life at some level, whether it is to please themselves or to achieve success as defined by others. At some point, people also wonder how they were made and why. They can either believe in the God of the Bible, who created them in love, or think that they are here by mere chance.

In Jesus, we find answers to all these questions. He is the way, the truth, and the life (John 14:6). Jesus illuminates all our questions, and living for Him becomes a joy filled with new excitement every day. By letting go and diving into the deep end, you receive the Holy Spirit as part of the package. Many Christians do not understand how significant this is or the power that comes with it.

In our next chapter, we will explore the power we have in Jesus through the Holy Spirit. A Christian should never be weak but powerful and mighty in Jesus' name.

Deepening Your Walk with Christ

Talking Points

1. Reflect on Philippians 1:21: What does it mean to you to say, "To live is Christ and to die is gain"?

2. Why do you believe that reading your Bible daily is essential?

3. Define "surrender" as it is explained in this chapter.

4. Based on this chapter, how would you describe a life fully surrendered to Christ?

5. What distinguishes a fan of Jesus from a true follower?

6. Read Matthew 16:25 and paraphrase its meaning in your own words.

7. What is the difference between a shallow-end follower and a deep-end follower of Christ?

8. Read John 14:26 and answer the following:
   (a) Who will the Father send to us?

   (b) Why did the Father send Him to us?

9. Are you willing to let God mold and shape you in order to walk as Jesus did? How do you think God is currently working on you?

10. Read Romans 12:1-3 and answer the following questions:
    (a) What are you called to present to God, and why?

    (b) What is being transformed in you, and why?

11. Read Romans 12:9 – 21 and make a list of "Do's" and "Do Not".
    DO   DO NOT

6

Unleashing the Holy Spirit's Potential

But you will receive power when the Holy Spirit has come upon you, and you will be my witnesses in Jerusalem and in all Judea and Samaria, and to the end of the earth. Acts 1:8

The Spirit-filled life is not a special, deluxe edition of Christianity. It is part and parcel of the total plan of God for His people. A. W. Tozer[ix]

One of the most transformative experiences for a follower of Christ is the power received at conversion. No other religion offers such a profound, supernatural power that can only be described as miraculous. In the NIV version of the Bible, the word "power" appears over 343 times[x], predominantly with two key meanings.

The first is "Dunamis," which denotes "a miraculous deed, something unique to the God of the Bible," and it is mentioned more than 117 times.[xi] The second term frequently used to denote power is "Exousia" (pronounced ex-oo-see-ah), appearing 103 times. This word signifies that "a person is given authority and the freedom to make decisions." Often, these two terms are used together.

For example, in Luke 9:1, as Jesus sent His disciples to preach the Gospel, He granted them Power (Dunamis) and Authority (Exousia) over all demons and to cure diseases. At conversion, the Bible states in 1 Corinthians 3:16 that our bodies become the temple of God and that the Holy Spirit now dwells within us. Additionally, Micah 3:8 proclaims that the Holy Spirit is omnipotent and omnipresent.

Psalm 139:7 also emphasizes that we cannot escape the presence of the Holy Spirit, who can act within us just as He acts within any other follower of Christ. This shared indwelling presence is what makes it so remarkable to connect with a believer from the other side of the world and feel an immediate kinship, as though you've known each other forever. The power of the Holy Spirit guides them just as He guides us, reinforcing an inescapable and profound truth.

It is important to remember that whenever you encounter the word "all" in the Bible, as mentioned in Luke 9:1, you should understand that "all means all," indicating that there is no greater extent beyond it. The Holy Spirit within us affirms this truth, and with His help, we can accomplish "all" things through Christ who gives us strength. This is only possible through the power of the Holy Spirit, as without God, we are incapable of doing anything.

In John 3:3, Jesus tells us that unless we are born again, we cannot see the kingdom of God. The very act of becoming born again at conversion is a supernatural work of the Holy Spirit, changing us by the power of God. Our old life is gone, and a new life has begun, as stated in 2 Corinthians 5:17. As Christians, we now live with the guidance of the Holy Spirit (John 16:13), washed and regenerated for God's purposes.

> *Titus 3:5 says "It's not by works of righteousness which we have done, but according to His mercy Jesus saved us, through the washing of regeneration and renewing of the Holy Spirit."*

Our good works and actions cannot bring us power, save us from ourselves, or protect us from eternal damnation. The power of the believer originates from the Kingdom of God, which cannot be accessed through the flesh, but only by the Spirit. Religion often emphasizes "doing things in the flesh" and adhering to rigorous rules that are impossible to keep. Such a focus will never bestow upon us the supernatural power that the Bible promises.

Christians who concentrate solely on what the flesh can control, like "good works," will never experience the manifestation of the Holy Spirit's power in their lives. By concentrating on what should not be done—which is the focus of many worldly religions—you will find yourself failing repeatedly. As we discussed in the previous chapter, Jesus came to save us from this futile lifestyle because we all fall short of the glory of God (Romans 3:23).

The reason so many people have left the church is due to Christians who live by the flesh, trying to follow religious rules and regulations, only to fail to meet those standards. Such Christians often become ultra-critical of others who do not follow Jesus in the way they believe is correct. This, my friends, is legalism, and it is not of God. This way of living will never produce the power of God within us.

Unfortunately, many Christians believe that merely following the rules makes us holy and good. However, if we truly focused on Jesus, who knows all the rules perfectly, our actions would naturally align with God's will. Focusing solely on the rules of religion is an attempt to control our outcomes through works. Romans 8:5 states, *"For those who live according to the flesh set their minds on the things of the flesh,"* which means relying on what we can control or do based on our own understanding of right and wrong. This mindset leads not to power but to failure and heartache. The verse continues, *"but those who live according to the Spirit set their minds on the things of the Spirit."*

Living according to the Spirit means spending quality time with Jesus and focusing on what the Spirit is guiding us to do. We should not make decisions based merely on what we think we are supposed to do, but rather act on what we know the Spirit is telling us to do. The Spirit will never lead us astray, but will always point us to Jesus, who is perfect in all things. True power comes from hearing and obeying the Spirit's direction, not from getting ahead of God by acting in the flesh based on our own judgments.

The Bible says in Mark 12:10 that Jesus is our Chief Cornerstone, and when we draw near to Him, all things are possible and our lives become unshakeable. Religion often focuses on rules to please God, which was never His intention. God desires true praise over sacrifice. In Psalms 69:30-31, David declares, *"I will praise the name of God with a song and will magnify Him with thanksgiving. This also shall please the Lord better than an ox or bull, which has horns and hooves."*

God wants His people to draw near to Him in a natural, sincere way that allows us to listen and obey His guidance. The word "obey" often trips up believers. If we truly understand that God is a good God and that He is for us and not against us, then obeying His instructions should be a joy, not a burden.

When we focus on living by rules, we are building our house on a weak foundation. When life hits us unexpectedly, we will crumble and fall. However, when we focus our lives on Jesus, we will withstand every storm because He is our Chief Cornerstone, our immovable rock, and our sure foundation.

> Luke 6:56-49 NKJV *"But why do you call Me 'Lord, Lord,' and not do the things which I say? Whoever comes to Me, and hears My sayings and does them, I will show you whom he is like: He is like a man building a house, who dug deep and laid the foundation on the rock. And when the flood arose, the stream beat*

vehemently against that house, and could not shake it, for it was founded on the rock.[a] But he who heard and did nothing is like a man who built a house on the earth without a foundation, against which the stream beat vehemently; and immediately it fell.[b] And the ruin of that house was great."

Living Beyond the Law in the Embrace of Grace

In the following chapters, we will look into how we can persevere when life challenges us by remaining focused on Jesus. This chapter emphasizes that our strength does not come from adhering to religious rules, but from drawing near to Jesus with the help of the Holy Spirit. We cannot transform ourselves from within; believing otherwise is a deception of Satan. While we can make better choices or seek rehabilitation, true inner change only occurs with the assistance of the Holy Spirit.

Consider Matthew 23:25 (ESV), where Jesus rebuked the Scribes and Pharisees: *"Woe to you, scribes and Pharisees, hypocrites! For you clean the outside of the cup and the plate, but inside they are full of greed and self-indulgence."* They were experts in following rules, which Jesus acknowledged in Matthew 5:20: *"unless your righteousness exceeds that of the scribes and Pharisees, you will never enter the kingdom of heaven."* Jesus recognized that living a perfectly holy life was the only way to enter the Kingdom of Heaven, and it was never about our efforts to achieve it. It has always been about Jesus and His actions, not ours.

By focusing on Jesus, we allow the Holy Spirit to guide us in fulfilling His desires for our lives, transforming us into His image. Unlike the Pharisees, who were preoccupied with external appearances, we achieve purity both inside and out through this divine transformation. It's not about our efforts, but rather our consistent pursuit of drawing near to God's perfect love manifested in His Son.

Following the rules should be a natural response to the leading of the Holy Spirit, not a precursor to it. Our efforts come only after we are led by the Spirit, not before. We often think we are being holy by adhering to "the Laws," but in reality, this distances us from Jesus and diminishes our power. When we focus our lives solely on Jesus, we are free from condemnation (Rom 8:1). Condemnation only arises when we attempt to save ourselves without the Holy Spirit's help.

The command is not to act first and then invite Jesus into our actions. Instead, we are called to "Be Still" and wait upon God, moving only when the Holy Spirit confirms the things of Jesus in our hearts. Everything the Holy Spirit does is to glorify Jesus and God. He will never lead us in any other direction. Serving Christ through our own abilities is utterly impossible; we rely on the Holy Spirit to empower us in our service to Christ.

Acts 1:8 states, *"You will receive power when the Holy Spirit has come upon you, and you will be my witnesses."* We cannot fully understand Jesus or possess true power (Dunamis) without the Holy Spirit. Tragically, many Christians today engage in ministry without the anointing of the Holy Spirit. The anointing is the power provided by the Holy Spirit, imbued with love and passion for others and the things of God. Ministry should never be burdensome or unbearable (Matthew 11:30).

In order to transform ourselves internally, we need the Holy Spirit to open our eyes to the teachings of Jesus. The only way to truly understand these teachings is by reading the Bible. Without daily engagement with God's word, we won't be able to discern what the Holy Spirit is communicating to us. If we remain unaware of His guidance, we will be devoid of the direction and power that Jesus possessed, rendering our ministry ineffective from the start.

We hear the Holy Spirit most clearly when we quiet our minds and eliminate worldly distractions. Prioritizing worldly matters and lifestyles over spiritual connection prevents us from being in tune with the Spirit. Experiencing the Holy Spirit's power to achieve divine acts requires us to consciously choose to maintain constant fellowship with the Father. Making life decisions without dedicating time to prayer, worship, and daily reading of God's word will lead to costly and unfruitful outcomes.

True spiritual power comes when we regularly quiet our minds before God, listen to His voice, and follow His guidance through obedient actions.

Attending church three days a week and reading your Bible daily does not guarantee that you have the power of the Holy Spirit. Remember, the Scribes and Pharisees were diligent in these practices, yet Jesus rebuked them. While these activities are commendable, they are pointless if not accompanied by listening to the Holy Spirit and obeying His guidance.

Many of us engage in ministry because we believe it is what God wants, but without the anointing of the Holy Spirit, our efforts are fruitless. It's often hard to recognize this when we're deeply involved in our work. By God's grace, I pray that as you read this, your eyes will be opened if you're in this situation. My hope is that God does for you what He did for me—strip you of your current identity, remove you from ministry as you know it, and humble you into submission to His refining process.

I am incredibly grateful for how God has transformed my life for His glory. Despite the challenges, I wouldn't change any of it. Experiencing the "power" (Dunamis) of the Holy Spirit within you is indescribable and beyond imagination. When God rules your life, your thoughts are clearer, your speech is purer, you are kinder, you love more deeply, and your relationships and ministry flourish.

If you feel you lack the Holy Spirit's power, I encourage you to be honest with yourself and trust that God's way is always better. Ask God to dismantle your current identity and allow Him to rebuild you in His way. It may be painful and challenging, but trust me, it's well worth it.

What kind of Power does the Holy Spirit give us?

To possess the power of the Holy Spirit is to possess the power of God. Imagine, if you will, that with God, anything is possible. This isn't mere imagination; it's a profound truth (Matthew 19:26). The Holy Spirit serves as our irreplaceable guide, perfect teacher, seal of our salvation, and comforter (John 14:16-18).

In the Old Testament, the Spirit empowered the Israelites to achieve supernatural feats beyond their natural abilities. This same Spirit is available to us, equipping us in ways we could never accomplish on our own. Embracing the Holy Spirit means stepping into a realm where divine possibilities become our reality.

> *Exodus 31:2-5 NIV says "See, I have chosen Bezalel son of Uri, the son of Hur, of the tribe of Judah, and I have filled him with the Spirit of God, with wisdom, with understanding, with knowledge and with all kinds of skill to make artistic designs for work in gold, silver and bronze, to cut and set stones, to work in wood, and to engage in all kinds of crafts."*

For Samson, the Holy Spirit gave him the strength to accomplish extraordinary feats, such as killing a lion with his bare hands (Judges 14:6). Trying to confine the Holy Spirit or thinking He is limited in any way is incredibly foolish. Our success is severely restricted without the involvement of the Holy Spirit. Conversely, our success becomes extraordinary when the Holy Spirit leads the way.

Let's look deeper into some of the remarkable powers granted to us by God through the indwelling of the Holy Spirit.

The Holy Spirit always guides believers to walk in the light of Christ. With the Holy Spirit as our guide, we can no longer follow paths that are not in our best interest. It is our flesh that often leads us astray. However, with the Holy Spirit guiding us, we gain insights that others around us cannot see; we are given the inside scoop.

Imagine yourself as the commander of an army with the responsibility to defeat the enemy. Now, envision having access to the enemy's detailed battle plan, which outlines their exact strategy against you. This information would keep you one step ahead, allowing you to surprise the enemy at every turn—they would never see you coming. This is what it's like having the Holy Spirit as our guide. We avoid the enemy's traps, and victory is assured.

The enemy will continually attempt to lure us with distractions to lead us off course. However, if we stay in the word, wait for the Holy Spirit's guidance, and obediently act on it, we will remain on the right path. To succeed in our daily lives, we need the constant guidance of the Holy Spirit. He truly does speak to us.

Learning to recognize the Holy Spirit's voice requires spending time with Him through prayer and reading the word of God. As your relationship with Him grows stronger, you will more easily recognize His still, small voice.

Paul mentioned in Philippians 4 that he learned to be content in whatever state he was in. Without contentment, we have no power over the enemy or his strongholds, hindering the Holy Spirit from guiding us effectively. As 1 Timothy 6:6 states, *"Godliness with contentment is great gain."*

Think of the commander of an army; if he lacks the patience to wait for his guide's direction, he would likely lose the battle, resulting in failure rather than gain. When we surrender and obey the Holy Spirit's directives, we will consistently experience success. Remember, God is perfect and always victorious. However, anxiety and restlessness only lead to defeat.

The Holy Spirit knows the perfect timing and method for our actions. Sometimes, His guidance can be immediate, while other times, it may take months or even years. If we are not content with the current moment God has placed us in, we essentially hand victory over to the enemy.

By trusting the Holy Spirit to guide us in everything, we can witness the enemy's swift retreat.

Another crucial area a commander must recognize to conquer his life through surrender is understanding the battle plans given to him. In the next chapter, we will explore what it means to be a warrior for God, focusing on being on the offense, not just defense. To achieve this, we must always understand the battle plan and be prepared to act when called upon.

At the moment of conversion, a Christian is indwelled by the Holy Spirit and receives access to every spiritual battle plan. The Holy Spirit teaches the Christian, in moments of need, the directives of their superior officer. The enemy is perpetually on the attack, and the Bible provides answers to every arrow he hurls at us. By studying the battle plan and knowing its intricacies, the Holy Spirit can remind us of its details whenever needed.

Imagine a commander heading into battle without knowing the battle plans. Now, imagine this commander has meticulously studied these plans and possesses perfect recall of them during combat. This is exactly what the Holy Spirit does for us—He enables us to win every battle we face. We will know precisely what to do in every situation if we are familiar with God's word. This is why reading and studying God's word is so essential.

Satan's Lies and Attacks

In Matthew 4:1-11, Jesus was tempted by Satan in the wilderness. Throughout these temptations, Jesus responded each time with the word of God. Although Satan tried to misuse the scriptures against Him, Jesus, well-versed in God's word, effectively countered every attack. It's crucial to recognize that Satan is highly clever and manipulative, employing every possible tactic to lead us astray.

When we face temptations, the Holy Spirit assists us by bringing the word of God to our minds. It's important to realize that the enemy cannot be defeated by our personal opinions or feelings. The enemy is overcome by the unwavering truth of God, and victory always comes through His word.

One significant area where Satan often targets believers is their minds. He deceives people into believing false realities, convincing them that earthly things are necessary to alleviate their pain. He lies, suggesting that Jesus is insufficient and manipulates the truth. Therefore, it's essential to immerse ourselves in God's word daily to resist Satan's deceptions effectively.

Many of our addictions stem from Satan's lies. To counteract these deceptions, we must learn to take every thought captive, as instructed in 2 Corinthians 10:5. This involves replacing negative thoughts with the truth of God's word. Our bad habits often cause us to seek short-term comfort, but over time, these false comforts can lead us away from God's perfect will for our lives. Although we wish to change, our ingrained habits can feel overpowering, leaving us feeling hopeless and as if nothing works.

In my book "Keys to Being Set Free," I explore various hang-ups that can hinder Christians from experiencing deeper intimacy with Jesus, often without them even realizing that these hang-ups exist.

One reason for this is that we've spent so much time focusing on our problems or rigid religious rules that we've distanced ourselves from the power of the Holy Spirit.

Our hang-ups develop gradually over time. If we don't address them promptly, they begin to control our habits. When these habits are not centered on and focused on Jesus, our lives can become chaotic and we find ourselves distant from God.

It is only through the Holy Spirit's guidance in our lives that we find healing, leading us to develop new habits that produce fruit through His power. If we commit to surrendering every thought when tempted and replacing negative thoughts with God's word, we will gradually see victory. While we may initially slip up as we unlearn bad habits, having a brother or sister in Christ to support us and keep our focus on Jesus can be invaluable. This is why we gather as the body of Christ—not to share opinions or feelings, but to guide each other back to Jesus in challenging times.

If you are struggling with hang-ups, I highly recommend going through my book "Keys to Being Set Free" with another believer to find true freedom from these issues and addictions. Additionally, this book "Conquer Through Surrender" will help establish a firm foundation, so that when you read "Keys to Being Set Free," you'll be one step closer to achieving intimacy with God.

Embracing the Transformative Power
of the Holy Spirit

The Holy Spirit will provide the strength to persevere, but you must commit to proclaiming God's truth daily. Each time you're tempted and capture that thought, replacing it with God's word, you move one step closer to freedom. Over time, your bad habits will diminish, and Jesus will increase within you. When the enemy tries to deceive you, your new habit of relying on God's truth will naturally counter his attacks. Ultimately, this will lead to your freedom.

The Holy Spirit provides us with whatever we need at the moment to defeat the enemy. If we need wisdom, He grants us wisdom. If we need strength, whether physical or mental, He supplies it. The Holy Spirit is instrumental in moving mountains in our lives. He empowers us to use our gifts and talents effectively. If a miracle is needed, and God intends to use it for His glory, it will happen.

God created us in His perfect likeness and has given us numerous weapons to use. It's unfortunate that many Christians never tap into this immense power, instead choosing to be gripped by fear. Despite having these capabilities, they often remain unused. God is always at work around us, and without the Holy Spirit opening our eyes to His actions, we would miss out on the incredible joy God brings us daily. The Holy Spirit is the ultimate power source connected to the Almighty God, and by tapping into Jesus daily, we have constant access to this power.

Everything we do should aim to bring glory to God. He has the plans, and He uses the Holy Spirit to execute them within our lives.

I'll conclude this chapter with a story that reminds me of the unexpected blessings and grace we receive in life.

There was once a girl named Sue who longed to attend her school prom but couldn't afford a new dress. Determined to go, she decided to make her own dress using whatever fabric scraps she could find. Although Sue had never made a dress before, she poured her heart into the project. When she finished, she proudly wore her handmade dress around school, eager to show her friends. Despite their best efforts, her friends struggled to hide their reactions, as the dress was far from beautiful. Nevertheless, Sue was proud of her creation, even though she still wished she could have purchased a new one.

Later that evening, a kind woman named Mrs. Mary, who had always been nice to Sue, stopped by her house with an invitation to go out. They visited Saks Fifth Avenue, where Sue was thrilled to see all the beautiful items. Mrs. Mary took her to a fashion show happening in the store. As models showcased stunning dresses, one dress in particular made Sue gasp. Mrs. Mary noticed Sue's admiration and saw the price tag marked at $4,000. Sue couldn't fathom how anyone could afford such an extravagant dress.

To her surprise, Mrs. Mary bought the dress for her without any explanation. She simply wanted Sue to look her very best, and it had nothing to do with what Sue had done or what she deserved. It was a gracious gift, given out of love and generosity.

As Christians, we often try to manage our lives on our own, but in the presence of Christ, we find ourselves spiritually bankrupt. We have nothing of true worth to offer Him except our hearts. Attempting to make ourselves presentable is almost laughable. The role of the Holy Spirit is much like that of Mrs. Mary in the story. He is responsible for making us truly beautiful. We can't earn or afford what He offers, but we can accept it freely.

The Holy Spirit protects us and helps us present our best selves before the almighty God. Our impatience often leads us to act like Sue, trying to piece together whatever we can to make sense of our lives. However, the Holy Spirit knows what's best and only desires to give us the very best if we wait on Him. When we surrender our lives to Jesus, we receive the Holy Spirit freely. With the Holy Spirit, we possess everything we need, including an inner and outer beauty that reflects God's glory.

In the next chapter, we will focus on engaging the enemy in battle and putting on the full armor of God.

Unleashing the Holy Spirit's Potential

Talking Points

1. Read 1 Corinthians 3:16 and answer the following:
   (a) What becomes the temple of God?

   (b) What does it mean to you to have the power of the Holy Spirit?

2. Explain the difference between following the rules of religion and following Jesus' promptings.

3. Describe what spending quality time with God looks like and what it means to you.

4. Explain the difference between a weak and a firm foundation.

5. Read John 14:16-18 and answer the following:
   (a) What is the definition of 'abide'?

(b) Who will abide with you, and for how long?

(c) Why can't the world receive the Holy Spirit?

6. What is the main purpose of the Holy Spirit?

7. In what ways can the Holy Spirit change you from the inside?

8. Share any experiences you have had with the power of the Holy Spirit in your life.

9. Read Matthew 4:1-11 and answer the following:
   (a) How did Jesus fight off the temptations of Satan?

   (b) How did Satan attempt to manipulate Jesus into these temptations?

Engaging the Enemy

"God is strong, and he wants you strong. So take everything the Master has set out for you, well-made weapons of the best materials. And put them to use so you will be able to stand up to everything the Devil throws your way. This is no afternoon athletic contest that we'll walk away from and forget about in a couple of hours. This is for keeps, a life-or-death fight to the finish against the Devil and all his angels." Ephesians 6:10-12 MSG

Engaging in Spiritual Battle: The Paradox of Victory in Surrender

In the journey to embody the essence of Christian life, we must acknowledge the ongoing spiritual battle we face as followers of Christ. This conflict unfolds in a world akin to enemy territory, where living our faith authentically demands courage and vigilance. We must equip ourselves daily to maintain our stance when challenged to defend our beliefs.

While Jesus' resurrection has dealt a significant blow to the adversary, diminishing his power, the threat he poses is far from extinguished. The enemy persists, relentless in his assaults. As I have shared in earlier chapters, Satan, described as 'the god of this world' in 2 Corinthians

4:4, once held dominion over us, until our salvation marked our freedom from his control. Our commitment to Christ signals to Satan that we are adversaries worth his full wrath. His agenda is clear: to prevent at all costs our alignment with God.

Seasoned Christians often say that the longer one lives the Christian life, the more joyful and meaningful it becomes as they have learned to navigate life's hardships. Yet, a stark contrast exists for the spiritual baby Christian. After embracing Christ, they may find the journey hard with towering challenges, where trials often overtake them.

Satan's most effective weapon to stop our spiritual progress is our own silence. Observing the contemporary Christian landscape, this silence is loudly apparent on pressing matters where dark influences seem to advance unchallenged. Like abortion, same-sex marriage, and woke theology amongst other things, but silence should not be our fallback. Rather than defaulting to a defensive posture, we must proactively confront these difficulties. Our might in this struggle, bolstered by our faith in Jesus, signals not just resistance but a promise of victory.

To concede our voice to the enemy is to grant him terrain in our personal lives and the collective spiritual landscape. May we never forget that in the unique strategy of God's Kingdom, our true conquest over darkness begins with the counterintuitive act of surrender to Christ. Through him, we are called not just to withstand, but to reclaim and triumph.

Satan is incredibly adept at diverting a believer's focus to everything around them. As followers of Christ, we no longer belong to Satan, and focusing on ourselves is precisely what he desires. Satan employs every tactic imaginable to shift our gaze from Jesus to our circumstances, feelings, or desires. He skillfully deceives us into justifying the thoughts in our minds, making us believe that we need what we feel. This deception grows into a desire that ultimately distances us from Jesus. When problems arise, we can no longer claim Jesus' victory over them because we have strayed too far from Him.

We were created for the pleasure of Jesus and are called to be bondservants of the Most High God. As His servants, we are meant to serve Him and live for Him in all that we do. When we focus on our problems or pursue what we think is best, we lose sight of our true purpose. Our perception of problems or needs is only relevant when seen through God's perspective. Just as Jesus desires all of us, Satan can exploit our passions, desires, and circumstances for his purposes and our defeat. Everything Satan offers is laced with deceptive evil, whereas everything Jesus wants for us is filled with God's goodness.

If we remain silent and fail to engage the enemy with the truth, it indicates that we are more focused on ourselves rather than on God's greater purpose for our lives.

Once Jesus saved us from our misery and offered us His hope and salvation, we should have died to ourselves. The Bible tells us that at conversion, we deny ourselves, pick up our cross, and follow Jesus (Matthew 16:24). Additionally, in 2 Timothy 2:3-4, we're reminded that conversion enlists us in the Lord's army, engaging us in spiritual warfare: *"You therefore must endure hardship as a good soldier of Jesus Christ. No one engaged in warfare entangles himself with the affairs of this life, that he may please him who enlisted him as a soldier."*

Whether or not we follow Christ, we will face hardships. The difference for believers is that by holding tightly to Jesus, we have hope amidst our trials. Often, Christians do not have the right view of themselves in the light of Christ. This book aims to help followers of Jesus see Him properly and recognize that we have been chosen to be His instruments in the spiritual battles on earth.

Jesus did not come to be served but to serve (Mark 10:45). He came to defeat Satan's deception that persuades humanity to live for themselves. Jesus didn't just save us from our sins and provide the resources to claim victory over them; He also came to defeat Satan. In John 14:12, Jesus tells His disciples that they will do even greater things than He did on this earth. He battled Satan in every conceivable way. If we are to do even greater things, then let the challenge begin.

Satan's Temptation to Silence My Life.

Before we look deeper into the details of engaging the enemy, I want to take a moment to discuss a significant area in my life where Satan attempted to silence me. I was raised in a Christian home and have attended church my entire life, but I had a flawed understanding of God.

In Deuteronomy 11:13-14, God tells the Israelites that if they obey His commandments, He will bless them with rain for their land and an abundance of grain and wine. Satan exploited this by making me question, "What happens when I fall short and do not obey His commands? Will He punish me like He did Israel?" When we are outside of Jesus, the answer is yes. But with Jesus, God sees us as perfect and no longer disobedient.

Satan deceived me so thoroughly that every time I failed, I would become utterly depressed and shut down. I closed myself off from everyone around me. Eventually, I would pick myself back up and strive for success, only to fall short again. As I mentioned in the last chapter, my eyes were constantly focused on the problem rather than the problem-solver, the Savior.

When we fix our eyes on the Savior, we no longer live by our performance but by His and what He is doing around us. Satan wanted me to focus on how flawed I was, which was very flawed. He convinced me that every time I failed, God was against me. THIS IS A LIE, a complete falsehood that many Christians easily believe. They fall into the trap of feeling they must justify themselves, which takes them out of the battle. This cycle keeps going endlessly, with Satan keeping us exactly where he wants us, endlessly chasing our tails, so to speak.

To engage the enemy and reclaim territory from Satan, we must break this cycle by learning to overcome his lies about us. Believing these lies led to my silence and passivity in my faith. God calls us to be active warriors on the battlefield, using our voices and discipling others who, in turn, will disciple others.

In Jesus, we are forgiven of our sins once and for all, but we remain accountable for them. While we are not condemned to death because of our sins, we will nevertheless face the consequences of our actions. The following section will explore how sin can hamper our efforts in our spiritual battle against the enemy. I will share my personal experience and how, by the grace of God, I have learned to overcome Satan's lies.

By learning to keep our eyes on Jesus in all circumstances, the grip of sin in our lives will loosen. Although we will never be entirely sinless, we will begin to sin less and less as we draw closer to Jesus. We will continually fall short of God's perfection until we reach heaven, but this does not mean that God is angry with us. His grace is truly sufficient and His love for us is pure without condemnation.

Engaging in Spiritual Warfare

Ephesians 6:12 reminds us that our battles are not against one another; our true conflict isn't with flesh and blood, despite Satan's attempts to make us believe otherwise. Instead, we contend with a spiritual host of darkness, wicked and vile forces opposed to everything of God.

The Message Bible elucidates Ephesians 6:10-12 beautifully: *"God is strong, and he wants you strong. So take everything the Master has set out for you, well-made weapons of the best materials. And put them to use so you will be able to stand up to everything the Devil throws your way. This is no afternoon athletic contest that we'll walk away from and forget about in a couple of hours. This is for keeps, a life-or-death fight to the finish against the Devil and all his angels."*

There's no sugarcoating this message: we are locked in a struggle against the forces of evil. With God's help, we can overcome them. This is an intense spiritual conflict, a life-or-death fight with no room for complacency. It's crucial to recognize that we have an enemy who seeks to destroy the joy we have found in Jesus. Satan harbors a deep hatred for Christ; unable to crucify Him again, he aims to destroy His followers.

To be in Christ means to be seated in the heavenly places, safe from Satan's ultimate grasp. Although Satan cannot destroy a true child of Jesus, he tirelessly tries to steal our joy and provoke us into thinking our battles are with people, rather than recognizing the spiritual nature of our struggles. Understanding this is crucial for seeing everything from God's perspective.

We must avoid getting entangled in physical confrontations with people or problems, realizing that these are always spiritual attacks. Surrender everything to Jesus and trust in Him, for in the flesh, no one can win a spiritual battle. Reacting hastily will only lead to defeat. Having the wrong perspective on our existence will mislead us whenever we face opposition. If we don't acknowledge that we are at war from the moment we wake up, Satan gains an advantage. However, if we wake up prepared for battle and focus on bringing glory to God, we will triumph greatly.

Viewing every circumstance from God's perspective provides a distinct advantage over evil. When we make situations about ourselves, we allow Satan to divert our attention from Jesus. It's always about Him, and in Jesus, we will always find our source of peace. Fighting physically against the flesh only leads to anger, bitterness, depression, hurt, confusion, and pain—all results of serving Satan. Nothing good comes from it. Instead, focus on the spiritual battle and rely on Jesus for true peace.

I don't know about you, but my flesh is most often tested by those closest to me—my wife, kids, and friends. Satan frequently uses these close relationships to try to bring us down because he despises a happy family and a strong marriage. His aim is to create disorder and alienation in every family. He seeks the total destruction of our relationships with family members and close friends.

Satan knows our daily routines and targets our vulnerabilities, which is why it's so important to be prepared. By being prepared, this allows us to be on the offensive. Ephesians 6:13, it says we should *"take up the whole armor of God, that we may be able to withstand in the evil day, and having done all, to stand."* But what does Paul mean by "the evil day"? This refers to our hour of darkness, the moment when the temptation to sin is strongest—when our opportunity and desire to sin converge.

In these moments, we desperately need the strength of the Lord. Without it, we risk hurting ourselves and those around us. Being armored with God's protection and prepared for these spiritual battles helps us withstand these attacks and maintain harmony in our lives and relationships.

Being tempted does not equate to sinning; experiencing temptation is a natural part of life. It is our actions resulting from that temptation that determine whether we sin. From a man's perspective, consider the difference between appreciating a woman's beauty and lusting after her. Simply acknowledging her beauty and moving on is not sinful, but repeatedly looking with impure intentions is. Temptation itself isn't the sin; it's the yielding to it that is.

Sin is anything that diverts our focus from Jesus' perfect will for our lives. It occurs when we prioritize our desires over what God knows is best for us. When we lose sight of God's goodness or fail to trust Him, we become susceptible to rebellion against His desires. Failing to view ourselves as spiritual agents of Jesus can cause us to falter in the face of temptation.

To overcome temptation daily, it's crucial to put on the full armor of God and maintain the right perspective. Without this spiritual readiness, we are likely to struggle. However, when we understand our identity in Christ and take our calling seriously, we gain the strength to withstand temptation and defeat Satan simultaneously.

Positioning yourself in situations where the temptation to sin is high makes maintaining holiness a very challenging task. We've all heard the saying, "If you're on a diet, don't go to the donut store." Similarly, when we align our daily walk with what we see Jesus doing, we gain the ability to discern His guidance.

For instance, if you're a man struggling with lusting after women at the beach, I believe God will guide you to places where such temptations are minimized. Walking with Jesus, following His pace and design, always positions us in strength, not weakness. Conversely, acting according to our flesh places us in positions of vulnerability.

This concept ties back to our motives chapter. If our intentions are self-serving rather than God-pleasing, we will constantly encounter opportunities to sin. There must be a transformation within us, an awakening of our soul, to fully grasp this truth. Living for oneself will never bring true peace and rest; it will only lead to more temptations and spiritual imbalance.

A true follower of Christ understands that living in accordance with what they see Jesus doing keeps them far from opportunities to sin.

Such a life leads to joy and harmony, rather than the discord that accompanies self-serving choices.

Temptation can lead to opportunities that evolve into desires, which in turn divert our focus away from Jesus. It is the desire for sin that forms our bad habits and addictions. When our sin reaches this level, we are in need of healing from Jesus. This is the point where repentance is crucial, requiring us to completely change course and move away from our sinful desires.

At this level of sin, we are often blinded to God's truths. Many individuals in this stage struggle to comprehend God's word and require the guidance of a mature Christian to help them refocus on Jesus. If you find yourself lost and yearning for God's ways, I encourage you to pray earnestly and seek out a mature Christian to walk this journey with you. I wrote my book, "Keys to Being Set Free," as a one-on-one discipleship curriculum to assist you along your journey to freedom.

My life, although not perfect as I am still learning every day, is a testament to what God's power can do in someone. It shows that your desires can be transformed and changed. My struggles were with greed and lust, but for others, it might be gluttony, debt, drugs, alcohol, or shopping. Satan has myriad ways to keep us preoccupied and destructive. Sadly, I spent many years at this stage, quick to justify that everything was fine and that my relationship with God was intact.

This is where a loving, mature Christian can play a vital role in helping us discern when we are falling for the enemy's lies. I have them in my life, their guidance can be instrumental in steering us back toward the truth and the freedom that comes from following Jesus.

> Galatians 6:1-2 "Brethren, if a man is overtaken in any trespass, you who are spiritual restore such a one in a spirit of gentleness,

considering yourself lest you also be tempted. Bear one another's burdens, and so fulfill the law of Christ."

Being overtaken by sin detracts us from fulfilling the Great Commission. The last thing Satan wants is for us to share the incredible news about Jesus with others. When we are overwhelmed with sin, we cannot fully pursue God's greatest commandment for our lives. In Matthew 28:19-20, Jesus instructs us to *"go and make disciples of all nations, and to baptize them in the name of the Father, Son, and Holy Spirit."* This is a direct command to Jesus' warriors, not a mere suggestion.

For a Christian, not sharing the love of Jesus should be unthinkable. If we aren't spreading His message, it's either due to a lack of opportunity or because sin in our life has silenced us through Satan's influence. The battle lines were drawn long ago, and there is an all-out war for the souls of mankind. Followers of Christ have been chosen to deliver the message of freedom and hope to everyone. It is our duty to remain vigilant, with eyes to see and ears to hear how God is moving around us. Many people are hurting, dying, and in desperate need of spiritual aid.

If we are weighed down by our own sins and not ready for battle each day, how can we assist others in being set free by the truth, particularly if we are not living by it ourselves? Yes, all have sinned and fallen short, but being absorbed in sin prevents us from engaging in God's calling for us. We will face evil days, but as followers of Christ, we have the choice to either surrender to Jesus or to the enemy. There is significant work left to be done. Let's engage in this mission, claim victory over the enemy, and refuse to retreat and be defeated.

To accomplish this, we need to comprehend how the armor of God functions and how we can utilize it to our advantage against the enemy. We will delve into this further in the next section.

Full Armor of God

We have established that our enemy possesses supernatural powers and that the battles we face are not against flesh and blood. The church is engaged in spiritual warfare, and the weapons used in this conflict are vastly different from those we employ in our everyday, worldly lives. While we may have an abundance of natural resources at our disposal, victory in these spiritual battles requires mighty spiritual weapons.

These divine weapons empower us to defeat the enemy when spiritual warfare arises, for without them, we would not stand a chance. We know that the enemy is highly intelligent and has a well-crafted strategy to destroy us. To overcome him, we need to equip ourselves with the full armor of God and maintain constant discernment to recognize the enemy in all his forms. Though he may disguise himself to appear good, we must rely on God's truth, as revealed in the Bible, to discern whether what we are hearing and seeing aligns with God's word.

We cannot afford to be mesmerized by appearances that contradict the word of God. The enemy is subtle in presenting evil and meticulously organized in his strategies. While some of us might be skilled in manipulating the truth, the enemy surpasses us in cunning and deceit. Therefore, we must be vigilant. As John 8:32 reminds us, *"We should know the truth, and the truth will set us free."*

In Isaiah 59:16 and the verses that follow, Isaiah portrays a vivid image of God preparing for battle. In verse 17, he describes God *"putting on righteousness as a breastplate and a helmet of salvation on His head."* This imagery provides the backdrop for Paul's description of the full armor of God in Ephesians 6. While many have interpreted Paul's depiction as referencing a Roman soldier, I believe he was actually alluding to Jesus himself, as mentioned in Isaiah 59.

By doing so, Paul aimed to show that Jesus wore this armor, tested its effectiveness, and proved beyond a doubt that it is trustworthy. Paul's message to his readers was meant to instill confidence and security in them. Although the enemy might paralyze us momentarily, wearing the full armor of God will enable us to stand firm, even in the darkest times of our lives.

Let's break down Ephesians 6:14-18 to understand how we can be properly prepared for battle, just as Jesus was. Putting on the full armor of God and choosing to walk in the Spirit is a daily commitment we must make upon waking.

In verse 14, Paul speaks of the **Belt of Truth**, which represents God's word as true. Every day, we must make a deliberate decision to meditate on what is true, and be steadfast in our hearts that what God says in His word is ultimate and true. The Belt of Truth keeps our minds pure, free from confusion, and aligned with God's word. John 14:6 tells us that Jesus is the truth, and when we focus on Him, we can successfully navigate times of deception.

The next piece of armor mentioned in verse 14 is the **Breastplate of Righteousness**. By putting this on daily, we repel Satan, the accuser of our brethren. His attempts to burden us with guilt over past sins are thwarted. We stand forgiven through the blood of Jesus, shielding our hearts from Satan's fiery darts. Although our past sins have the potential to cripple us, they no longer hold the power to defeat us.

> Proverbs 4:23, says: *"Above all else, guard your heart, for everything you do flows from it."*

This verse is often interpreted to mean that the heart is the source of life and moral compass, and thus it's crucial to protect it from negative influences and sin. The heart is seen as the seat of emotions, desires, and thoughts, and guarding it can involve being mindful of what one accepts or engages in, such as the kind of media consumed, the company one keeps, and the thoughts one entertains.

Satan will continuously accuse us of our past mistakes and current shortcomings, causing these wounds to stay deep within our hearts. However, each day, we can remind him of Christ's righteousness. We do not serve our past mistakes; we serve the righteousness of Christ. When Satan attacks our hearts, we can declare that Jesus died for our sins and that His impenetrable armor now covers us. We stand in Christ's righteousness, which is a breastplate Satan cannot penetrate. Amen!

The third piece of armor, mentioned in verse 15, is the shoes of readiness: *"Having **shod your feet** with the preparation of the gospel of peace."* By wearing this armor, we signal to Satan that we are part of the Lord's army and will follow wherever God leads. This means relinquishing control over our day and aligning our steps with what Jesus is doing. We choose to be content, ready to move at His pace and for His purpose, demonstrating His peace to the world by showing His love, so others may come to Him. Being ready daily is our declaration of trust in Jesus with our lives.

The fourth piece of armor, found in verse 16, is the **Shield of Faith**: *"Above all, taking the shield of faith with which you will be able to quench all the fiery darts of the wicked one."* Each day, we mentally prepare to stay the course, regardless of the fiery darts aimed at us. Our Shield of Faith protects us from worry and doubt, reinforcing that Jesus is for us and will work all things together for our good, as stated in Romans 8:28. Paul uses the analogy of fiery darts to illustrate how Satan's attacks can come from anywhere, catching us off guard. If we are not properly guarded, an attack can set our minds ablaze with turmoil. The Shield of Faith comforts our minds, reminding us to keep our eyes on Jesus and proclaim that we belong to Him. Don't give up, don't give in—stay the course. God's got this, believe it.

The fifth piece of armor mentioned in verse 17 is the **Helmet of Salvation**. In Matthew 19:23-26, Jesus speaks to His disciples about how difficult it is for a rich man to enter the kingdom of heaven, comparing it to a camel passing through the eye of a needle. Astonished, the disciples ask, *"Then who can be saved?" Jesus replies, "With man this is impossible, but with God all things are possible."*

Satan will often try to deceive believers by convincing them they are not truly saved, preying on their imperfections and sins. However, apart from Jesus, salvation is indeed impossible—but if we are in Christ and He is in us, we are saved. Don't succumb to Satan's lies that question your salvation. You don't need to continually give your life over to Jesus; once you surrender, you are His.

In John 15:16, John reminds us that we did not choose Jesus, but He chose us first. With this in mind, how can we doubt our salvation when Jesus has given it to us freely despite knowing our shortcomings beforehand?

The sixth piece of armor, also found in verse 17, is the **Sword of the Spirit**, which is the word of God. Unlike the other pieces of armor intended for defense, this weapon is designed to be swung and used often. The Sword of the Spirit, as demonstrated by Jesus during His temptation in the wilderness, is supremely effective and life-changing. When we feel lost or have failed, God's Word brings us clarity and rejuvenates our spirit.

When Satan fills our minds with doubt and worry, counter him with the truth of God's Word. Speak it out loud, be relentless in your declaration of God's promises—keep wielding the Sword of the Spirit until you've beaten Satan into submission. Don't give him a moment's break; be ruthless in proclaiming God's truth, and I assure you, you will achieve victory.

The final weapon mentioned in verse 18 is one that I use as much if not more than, the Sword of the Spirit: Prayer. Paul urges us to *"pray always with all prayer and supplication in the Spirit, being watchful to this end with all perseverance and supplication for all the saints."* He emphasizes the importance of being in constant prayer, not just for ourselves but for all believers and the lost in this world. My wife and I make it a point to be present in public places each week specifically to pray for those around us. We feel it is our responsibility to be a light to others and remain available for whatever God desires us to do.

Prayer makes Satan quake in his boots. When we pray, we unleash spiritual weapons of mass destruction on everything he is trying to accomplish. There is no defense against prayer to Almighty God.

The last thing Satan wants is praying Christians. I encourage you to find within yourself the drive to pray often and fervently. Do you want to win and engage the enemy effectively? If so, get on your knees and don't get up until you sense God's guidance. Let's not give Satan any more ground. Instead, let's push him back fiercely and claim victory in Jesus' name!

Having established a solid foundation in the previous chapters on how to conquer through surrender, our next chapter will guide us on how to thrive even amidst great trials and tribulations.

ENGAGING THE ENEMY
Talking Points

1. Read Ephesians 6:10-12 in the Message Bible and respond to the following questions:
   (a) Who wants to make you strong?

   (b) What has He provided for you, and why?

   (c) How will you be able to stand against the Devil?

2. Reflect on your experience with the Christian Life: Have you found it joyful and meaningful or more difficult and challenging? Explain your perspective.

3. Identify areas in your life where you can more effectively engage the enemy.

4. Consider the influence of Satan: Has he ever made you believe that God is mad at you when you sin? Explain your experience.

5. Read Matthew 16:24 and describe what it means to you in your own words.

6. Provide an example of how we should respond to someone who offends us.

7. Identify areas in your life that tempt you and discuss strategies to avoid those temptations.

8. Address habitual sin: Are you struggling with a habitual sin? What steps are you taking to remove it from your life?

9. Read Ephesians 6:10-20 and answer the following:
   (a) If Christians are not to battle against flesh and blood, then who are we fighting against?

   (b) List the items of the Armor of God and describe their purposes in your own words:

10. Explain the importance of putting on the full armor of God daily. What steps are you taking to do so?

8

Strength in Times of Trial

James 1:2-4 *"Consider it a sheer gift, friends, when tests and challenges come at you from all sides. You know that under pressure, your faith-life is forced into the open and shows its true colors. So don't try to get out of anything prematurely. Let it do its work so you become mature and well-developed, not deficient in any way."* MSG

This verse sets the tone for this chapter, helping us to understand that, from God's perspective, trials are not bad but beneficial to us. Are trials enjoyable? Of course not! But if you desire to truly walk, talk, and act like Jesus, then you will inevitably face various trials as you are being sculpted. To fully understand Jesus's perfect will in our lives, God must first eliminate many of the bad habits that hinder our holiness before Him. We will face trials with or without Jesus. However, when we face them with Jesus, we are transformed into His image.

Many Christians struggle because we tend to fight the trials we encounter. As a result, we never fully mature in our walk and become a hypocritical mess, with one foot in the world and one foot with God. Our Christian life then becomes masked and devoid of the Holy Spirit's power. By allowing trials to run their course, the mask we hide behind is replaced with what God has planned for our lives. You will take on a new image, His image. Over time, and through many trials, you will begin to talk and act more like Jesus.

I read a statement from Oswald Chambers in my Utmost for His Highest[(xii)] devotional on trials. He said, "Suppose God tells you to do something that is an enormous test of your common sense, totally going against it. What will you do? Will you hold back? If you get into the habit of doing something physically, you will do it every time you are tested until you break the habit through sheer determination. And the same is true spiritually. Again and again, you will come right up to what Jesus wants, but every time you will turn back at the true point of testing until you are determined to abandon yourself to God in total surrender. Yet we tend to say, "Yes, but— suppose I do obey God in this matter, what about...?" Or we say, "Yes, I will obey God if what He asks of me doesn't go against my common sense, but don't ask me to take a step in the dark.""

Jesus Christ demands the same unrestrained, adventurous spirit in those who have placed their trust in Him that the natural man exhibits. If a person is ever going to do anything worthwhile, there will be times when he must risk everything by his leap into the dark. In the spiritual realm, Jesus Christ demands that you risk everything you hold on to or believe through common sense, and leap by faith into what He says. Once you obey, you will immediately find that what He says is as solidly consistent as common sense.

By the test of common sense, Jesus Christ's statements may seem mad, but when you test them by the trial of faith, your findings will fill your spirit with the awesome fact that they are the very words of God. Trust completely in God, and when He brings you to a new opportunity of adventure, offering it to you, see that you take it. We act like pagans in a crisis— only one out of an entire crowd is daring enough to invest his faith in the character of God".

Trials and tribulations are words that we do not like to hear. We all face different challenges and difficulties. But as Oswald Chambers says, we can either react like pagans in a crisis, or we can trust in the good and faithful character of God.

Many of us will face various forms of trials throughout our lives—whether they are financial, physical, familial, or relational. Each of us seems to have some "cross to bear." Some people hold the belief that becoming a Christian will eliminate all these trials, often referred to as the "prosperity gospel." This ideology suggests that faith in Jesus will lead to a life free of troubles. However, this notion is not supported by Scripture. On the contrary, Jesus made it clear that following Him would be challenging and fraught with difficulties.

In our lives, we encounter trials where God's hand may be evident, and we trust that He has a greater purpose for our struggles. However, there are also those prolonged trials where God's involvement is not as obvious, and the difficulties seem unending. It is in these moments that our faith is most severely tested. Our resolve and hope in Jesus may start to waver. We can begin to feel like the Israelites in the wilderness, wondering if the hardships we face make life more unbearable than the comfort of our previous circumstances.

During such times, we may find ourselves questioning God, asking "why" at every turn, and doubting His purpose and presence in our lives. This leads to a crisis of belief, forcing us to make a crucial decision: to fully surrender to God or to begin doubting His role in our lives. If we allow doubt to take root, we risk becoming like the Israelites—bitter and hard-hearted, perpetually wandering in our own wilderness of discontent and mistrust.

Thus, the journey through trials can either strengthen our faith and bring us closer to God, or lead us further away, depending on how we choose to respond to the tribulations we face.

For followers of Christ, trials are the very means through which God tests our resolve and draws us closer to Him. These trials serve as a divine pruning process, helping us *"bear much fruit,"* as stated in John 15. In Exodus 20:4-6, we learn that *"God is a jealous God"* who desires an intimate relationship with His children. Often, He uses trials to capture our attention and deepen our faith.

Some people claim that their lives are free of trials and that everything is going smoothly. To such assertions, one might question their veracity and, more importantly, their spiritual alignment. According to James 2, trials are inevitable for true children of God. No one enjoys the refining process that trials bring. Finding joy in the midst of suffering is particularly challenging, especially when it feels like there is no immediate end in sight.

However, what if we trained ourselves to perceive trials from God's perspective? Could we then find true joy and peace amidst our struggles? Jesus addresses this in John 16:33: *"I have said these things to you, that in me you may have peace. In the world you will have tribulation. But take heart; I have overcome the world"* (ESV).

Are we willing to let go of any preconceived notions about the kind of trials we might face and trust Jesus completely? Can we truly accept Isaiah 55:8-9, which reminds us that God's ways and thoughts are far above our own?

> *"For my thoughts are not your thoughts, neither are your ways my ways, declares the LORD. For as the heavens are higher than the earth, so are my ways higher than your ways and my thoughts than your thoughts"* (Isaiah 55:8-9, ESV).

Entrusting our lives to God's direction means embracing His higher wisdom and finding peace in His sovereignty, even when we do not fully understand the trials we are going through. By doing so, we open ourselves to experiencing the true joy and peace that Jesus promises, despite the inevitable tribulations.

These questions have been deeply ingrained in my mind as I have meditated on God's word. If I was going to grow in my walk with Jesus, I had to confront these questions with complete honesty. As a Christian, it is your responsibility to reflect on these questions as well. We have a choice: either we accept everything that God is doing in our lives without complaint, or we risk staying in a state of spiritual stagnation, much like the Israelites who remained in the wilderness due to their disobedience.

Many believers have grown up with the notion that God is solely a "blessing God." We often think that if we continue to walk righteously and perform good works amidst our trials, God will teach us valuable lessons and eventually bless us in return. We believe that trials are temporary, something to be endured just for a season and that blessings will inevitably follow. For example, if our trial is financial, we expect a blessing of money; if it involves relationships, we anticipate a new relationship or reconciliation; if it's circumstantial, we look forward to a resolution. We've been conditioned to see everything bad in our lives as a trial and everything good as a blessing from God.

But what if this understanding is limited? What if everything that we perceive as good could actually serve as a trial, and what if what we see as bad could truly be a blessing? Could this be true of God's ways?

This perspective challenges us to reconsider our assumptions about God's workings in our lives. Perhaps trials and blessings are not as black and white as we have been led to believe. Trials could be disguised blessings, drawing us nearer to God, and teaching us deeper reliance, patience, and faith. Conversely, what we perceive as immediate blessings might also come with their own set of challenges, requiring us to grow in new ways.

Ultimately, embracing this nuanced understanding of trials and blessings requires a shift in our spiritual perspective. It invites us to trust in God's higher wisdom, which transcends our limited human understanding. Are we willing to accept that God's ways are higher than our ways, and His thoughts are higher than our thoughts? Are we ready to see our lives through the lens of divine purpose, where both trials and blessings are part of His perfect plan for us?

Reflecting on these questions and accepting the complexities of God's workings in our lives can lead us to a deeper, more resilient faith. This mindset allows us to navigate life's challenges with greater peace and understanding, knowing that in all things, God is at work for our good.

> *Romans 8:28 (ESV) states, "And we know that for those who love God, all things work together for good, for those who are called according to His purpose."*

The term "good" in this context refers specifically to matters that are spiritual and eternal. This definition of "good" doesn't imply a material blessing or an escape from difficulties, nor does it refer to suddenly receiving a large sum of money. Instead, it signifies that regardless of the situation—be it favorable or adverse—God is working behind the scenes to bring glory to Himself, thereby amplifying His eternal perspective. For instance, consider a Christian prisoner of war who has spent much of his life in captivity and eventually dies in a concentration camp. In such a dire situation, would you tell him, "Hey brother, God's got your back, and this will ultimately turn out for the good, so keep the faith?"

Consider how the POW might perceive this statement. Does he cling to the hope that God will liberate him? Does he imagine one day having an incredible testimony to share? Perhaps he does. But what happens when he confronts the reality that escape is not an option? Will he still believe that his suffering is for his good and God's glory? If he truly sees his situation from God's perspective, then the answer is a resounding Yes. However, the answer could also be No, especially if his belief is rooted in the notion that God is solely a "blessing" God, focused on providing outcomes that align with his desires.

It's crucial to understand that once we commit our lives to Jesus, our existence is no longer about us, but about Him. Our outcomes are determined by what He deems best for His glory, both in our lives and beyond. Attempting to discern what we think is best for us is ultimately futile. Only God truly knows what is best, and He never makes mistakes.

God has called every believer for one singular purpose, to "thrive in our moment" so that He is glorified. I will elaborate more on this in later chapters. God has not called us to worry about our circumstances but to draw near to Him. He has not called us to fret over our position in life but rather to clear our minds so that we may remain in His presence. God does not view our circumstances as inherently good or bad; He sees them as opportunities for His glory to be revealed. The universe is designed to reflect His glory, and we, being made in His image, are to emulate Him. Our perspective should align with Jesus's: *"I am about my Father's business, and I only do what I see my Father do"* (Luke 2:49).

Focusing too much on our circumstances can shift our gaze from Jesus to the negative outcomes we anticipate. Doing so makes it challenging to embody Jesus's teaching to "only do what we see our Father doing." Often, we interpret our trials and circumstances as "hate" rather than "love," as "inconvenient" rather than "timely." In doing so, we forget that the Father operates solely out of love. We tend to see things in black and white—if something is bad, we expect God to make it good; if something is good, we consider it a blessing. However, God views all things as potential blessings through which His perfect will is enacted. He will use any circumstance in our lives to ensure that He is ultimately glorified.

So, if God's perfect will is being done, why did He allow the POW to die in captivity without rescuing him? Only the person facing such a circumstance can truly discern what God is asking of them. Take Paul, for example; he viewed his imprisonment as an opportunity to write, pray, and share the love of Jesus with everyone he encountered. Paul recognized that God controlled his circumstances, placing him in situations where God would be most glorified. He relinquished control over his life, aligning his actions with the will of his Father, and did nothing on his own. Paul learned to see his situation from God's perspective, rather than through the lens of the world.

We must understand that God is love, and everything He does in our lives is a reflection of that love. He desires fellowship with us and does not wish for even one person to be lost. Each challenge or trial we face is part of His plan to involve us in His greater purpose. Let us not be calloused like the Israelites; all God was doing was preparing them to be set apart, so the world would recognize Him as God.

If things in your life seem bad, understand that, in God's eyes, they are not bad but rather good. Train yourself to see them as God sees them. Persevere, knowing that God is at work and His love for you is unmistakable. He is refining you towards perfection.

If you are experiencing blessings, such as winning a million dollars, recognize that it is not about you. That wealth has been entrusted to you for His greater purpose. It is not merely for purchasing a new house or indulging in material things but for fulfilling His will, which requires seeking His guidance. Whatever the purpose, it will always lead us to the cross and deepen our desire for intimacy with our Abba Father.

God is Able, and God is Good

We must never lose sight of the fact that our God is good and that the trials we endure are for our good and His glory. Always remember

Philippians 1:6 (ESV): *"He who began a good work in you will bring it to completion at the day of Jesus Christ."* Jesus has a plan, and He will never leave you nor forsake you. Hold on and stay the course.

As it says in 2 Chronicles 20:12 (ESV), *"O our God, will you not execute judgment on them? For we are powerless against this great horde that is coming against us. We do not know what to do, but our eyes are on you."*

Our lives encompass a variety of roles and responsibilities. We are moms, dads, friends, pastors, politicians, business owners, or coworkers. Each of us has a role and a purpose, and opposition is inevitable. Many of us can relate to the sentiment expressed in the verse above.

The Bible repeatedly instructs us to keep our eyes on Jesus, with Matthew 6:33 being one of the most well-known verses: *"Seek first the kingdom of God, and all these things will be added to you."* Seeking God "in all things" means doing so not only in specific settings, such as at work or church but in every aspect of our lives.

What trials are we facing that are outside of our control? It could be a difficult spouse, a rude coworker, a friend who has betrayed you, or an impossible boss. Maybe we run our own business and are currently facing numerous tough decisions—vendors are upset, customers are angry, and employees are dissatisfied. We mentally acknowledge that we need help and are clueless about how to fix the situation. In our desperation, we might cry out to God, praying for swift intervention. We might say, "Please God, help me. I can't take this anymore. Lord, why is this happening? Why are you allowing me to go through this? This is not fair, Lord; I have done nothing wrong to deserve this." Yet, in all our crying out, we often forget to rest in Jesus.

Remember what I mentioned at the beginning: we must never lose sight that our God is good and that the trials we endure are for our good and His glory. Always keep in mind Philippians 1:6 (ESV), *"He who began a good work in you will bring it to completion at the day of Jesus Christ."* Jesus has a plan for your life. This plan includes guiding you through these trials and using them for His greater glory. Trust in His process, and find rest in His presence.

> *Deuteronomy 31:6 ESV says "Be strong and courageous. Do not fear or be in dread of them, for it is the Lord your God who goes with you. He will not leave you or forsake you."*

By not resting in Jesus we are putting the weight of our trial on our own shoulders.

> *Matthew 11:28-30 ESV says" Come to me, all who labor and are heavy laden, and I will give you rest. Take my yoke upon you, and learn from me, for I am gentle and lowly in heart, and you will find rest for your souls. For my yoke is easy, and my burden is light."*

When we carry those heavy burdens we also forget to wait on the Lord.

> *Psalms 46:10 "Be still, and know that I am God."*

We are called to wait patiently on the Lord, trusting that He is ultimately in control. He will resolve the problem according to His will, His purpose, and in His timing. So, when trials come, we must immediately surrender the problem to the Lord in prayer and wait for His prompting and direction. Our role is not to become impatient, emotional, or upset, nor is it to take control and figure out how to fix the situation ourselves. With our limited understanding, we truly have no idea what is best. Instead, we should rely on God and His infinite wisdom to guide and lead us.

Relying on God and His infinite wisdom to guide us can appear in numerous ways, as every situation is unique. From my experience, God often approaches each circumstance differently and seldom handles things the same way twice. His answers typically come in unexpected forms, ensuring that all glory goes to Him rather than to our own efforts.

For example, consider the story of King Jehoshaphat in 2 Chronicles 20. The Israelites faced a formidable enemy from Syria, inducing great fear in Jehoshaphat and his people. Instead of panicking or rushing into a decision, Jehoshaphat sought God's wisdom. He wisely called for collective prayer and fasting among the people, seeking divine direction. In verse 6, Jehoshaphat acknowledges God's sovereignty and goodness, reminding Him of His promises to Israel.

As they prayed, the spirit came upon Jahaziel, a Levite, who assured them not to fear the upcoming battle because it was not theirs but God's. This promise was crucial: the battle does not belong to us but to God. I will share more details about this divine guidance, but it's important to note the essence of the promise. When we surrender our worries and wait upon the Lord, His spirit guides us.

Our past experiences, whether influenced by our own efforts or by spiritual guidance, do not dictate our present or future. We must remember that every challenge belongs to God, and our role is to follow His instructions.

Our walk with God is deeply connected to our ability to hear Him speak. For many, the tendency to rely on control and intellectual solutions is all we know. When we operate this way, our motives can become clouded, making it difficult to discern God's direction. This doesn't mean that God cannot intervene in our moments of selfishness. His grace is boundless, and He often steps in with divine intervention at His perfect timing.

However, our impatience and unwillingness to wait on God significantly hinder our spiritual growth. Our purpose isn't to chase personal happiness or fulfill our own desires; we exist to bring glory to God through our lives. When we cling to controlling motives and a take-charge attitude, we distance ourselves from God. This separation makes it challenging to find true rest amid our trials.

If we find ourselves unable to hear from God, it could be because we haven't fully surrendered our will, past, thoughts, or ways to Him. As children of God, we are His property, bought with His blood, and we are no longer responsible for the outcomes of our lives. Romans 8:28 reminds us that *"God works all things together for the good of those who are called according to His purpose."* So, if God assures us that everything happening in our lives is working together for our good, we must trust Him.

Consider Daniel as he awaited his fate in the lion's den. He likely felt some nervousness, but he also trusted that God would work everything out for his good. Daniel knew that whether he lived or died, he was in God's hands. In his case, God chose to save him. As God's children, we can take comfort in the fact that when situations are tough, God sees what is best for our lives. Enduring trials can draw us closer to Him. The process may be painful, uncomfortable, or undesirable, but resisting God only prolongs our discomfort.

Instead, let go and allow Him to have His perfect way in your life. In the end, your joy will overflow, and you will be filled with an indescribable love for Jesus. Remember, God is able, and God is good!

Remember how I mentioned that God might not answer you in the way you expect? In Jehoshaphat's case, that was certainly true. God instructed Jehoshaphat to put his worship band at the front lines of the battle. It sounds surprising, right? Leading a worship band into a battle? Yes, exactly that!

Sometimes, all we need to do is worship Jesus, and He will handle the rest. In Jehoshaphat's situation, as the worshipers sang and praised, the enemy forces turned on each other and were completely defeated. All of this transpired while Jehoshaphat's people focused on worshiping God.

So, worship God now. Give Him praise, thank Him for the trials you face, and view them as opportunities to bring Him glory. In the next chapter, we will discover the significance of finding contentment through simple living. We will learn that adopting this lifestyle can help us resist the temptations Satan hurls at us during our trials.

Strength in Times of Trial

Talking Points

1. Read James 1:2-4 and answer the following:
   (a) What do trials in our lives produce?

   (b) Why must we allow patience to have its work within us?

   (c) Why are trials beneficial for us rather than harmful?

2. Read John 15:1-8 and answer the following:
   (a) Who is the Vine?

   (b) What happens to the branches that do not bear fruit?

   (c) What happens to the branches that bear fruit, and why?

   (d) Write out and memorize John 15:5

3. Provide an example of a trial where you resisted God's will.

4. Provide an example of a trial where you surrendered to God, allowing Him to work in you.

5. How did you grow closer to the Lord during your trial?

6. Read John 16:33 – What does Jesus mean when He said He overcame the world?

7. What does the phrase "I am about my Father's business and I only do what I see my Father do" mean to you?

8. What is the definition of long-suffering and what does that mean to you?

9. What advantages does a Christian have by letting God lead during a trial?

The Art of Contentment: Finding Peace in Simplicity

I am not saying this because I am in need, for I have learned to be content whatever the circumstances. I know what it is to be in need, and I know what it is to have plenty. I have learned the secret of being content in any and every situation, whether well-fed or hungry, whether living in plenty or in want. I can do everything through him who gives me strength. Philippians 4:11-13

For followers of Christ to *Conquer Life Through Surrender*, it requires us to embrace a life of simplicity. In this chapter, we will explore key questions: What does it mean to be content? How do we live without constant want?

In a world driven by the constant pursuit of bigger, better, and more, achieving simplicity can be challenging. Western culture, in particular, is notorious for its relentless push to buy new and improved products, teaching us to never be satisfied. Commercials and news reports seldom highlight the virtues of a simple life. Instead, they promote messages like "buy more," "get more," and "become more." This cultural pressure to acquire and achieve more can lead to significant stress in our lives.

The world rarely values the idea of letting things go, especially when desires are unmet. This mindset sets a precedent in our minds, creating standards that often conflict with God's principles. Without realizing it, we buy into the notion that more is better and inadvertently start living in a way that pleases only ourselves. This pursuit of self-fulfillment clouds our path to true contentment, leading us down dark alleys filled with broken promises.

In this chapter, we aim to understand how to find contentment and live simply, aligning our desires with God's will rather than the world's expectations. This journey involves recognizing the false allure of constant acquisition and learning to find joy and satisfaction in what truly matters.

I have discovered two important truths about the notion of "more." Firstly, a mentality focused on acquiring more will inevitably bring an abundance of additional problems. Secondly, a content and simple approach to life will lead to much greater peace. Interestingly, regardless of the path we think we're on, God has always been in control.

> *Proverbs 16:9 (MSG) states, "We plan the way we want to live, but only God makes us able to live it."*

For some, this might be a surprising realization: God ultimately determines the life we live. While we may believe we are in control, this verse reminds us that we can achieve nothing without His enablement. Throughout most of my early adult life, I pursued what seemed natural without realizing that God was leading me all along. It was only later that I understood He had been planning my course in spite of my own strenuous efforts.

As you read in the chapter on motives, my early life was dominated by a "more" mentality. My focus was entirely on achieving as much success as possible by the world's standards. This mindset led me down paths that hurt others and damaged relationships with friends I deeply cared about. My failure to live simply distanced me from Christ, clouding my vision and preventing me from clearly hearing and seeing God.

> Proverbs 10:9 *"The fear of the LORD is the beginning of wisdom, and the knowledge of the Holy One is insight."*

This verse teaches us that wisdom comes from fearing God and being obedient to His guidance. By embracing a simple lifestyle, we gain insight into the Holy One's perspective. Without this, our decision-making lacks divine insight, leaving us to rely on our limited understanding instead of God's infinite wisdom. When our pursuit of things isn't grounded in seeking and waiting upon Him, we end up acting without recognizing His presence and grace at work.

Living simply opens our eyes to see Jesus and enables us to thrive in any circumstance. It also brings great joy, reminding us that He has always been there. A content and simple life is crucial for navigating the highs and lows of life. We are no longer controlled by the world's pressures to please ourselves. As Philippians 4:11 states, *"Not that I speak in regard to need, for I have learned in whatever state I am, to be content."* Christ's message to His followers is to rest in Him, be content, and trust His timing and guidance.

Our culture often teaches us to take matters into our own hands, to trust in ourselves, and to do whatever it takes to get ahead, regardless of the consequences. From the world's point of view, it's a "do whatever it takes to get ahead" and "you snooze, you lose" mentality. However, in God's kingdom, patience is celebrated.

Living a content life encourages us to wait upon God to initiate things, allowing us to see His presence clearly in every aspect of life. This mindset is far more rewarding than constantly striving to make things happen on our own. Our impatience and unrealistic expectations have led to lives of bondage, filled with resentments, pressures, and stress—far from the joyful life God intended for us.

Hebrews 13:5 reminds us, *"Let your conduct be without covetousness; be content with such things as you have. For He Himself has said, 'I will never leave you nor forsake you.'"* When we choose a lifestyle of contentment, it reflects Jesus within us and serves as a testimony to others of our complete trust in Him.

Jesus never prioritized material possessions. Everything He had was a byproduct of what His Father was doing. His life was simple, driven by a purpose to please His Heavenly Father. This is the cost of being a disciple of Jesus. By giving our lives to Him, we relinquish our attachment to the world's standards of "much more."

In Matthew 8:18-20, a teacher of the Law told Jesus he would follow Him wherever He went. Jesus' response was true to His character, emphasizing the simplicity and focus required to follow Him.

> [18] *"When Jesus saw the crowd around him, he instructed his disciples to cross to the other side of the lake.* [19] *Then one of the teachers of religious law said to him, "Teacher, I will follow you wherever you go."* [20] *But Jesus replied, "Foxes have dens to live in, and birds have nests, but the Son of Man[a] has no place even to lay his head." Matthew 8:18-22 NLT*

Jesus never prioritized material wealth or desires as the world understands them. He viewed circumstances through a divine perspective, focusing on His mission to do whatever He saw His Father doing. As a result, His needs were always met. Often, we mistakenly prioritize material things, diverting our focus from what our Heavenly Father is doing.

A disciple of Jesus is saved from hell and granted eternal life. As the Bible says, we are in the world but not of it. Our lives are meant to glorify God, and He never intended for us to live for the world's comforts. Therefore, we should not make them our priority. Adopting the world's standards of "much more" hampers our ability to walk intimately with Jesus.

Consider what Jesus told the rich young ruler to do with his wealth in Matthew 19. This serves as a powerful reminder that true discipleship involves shedding material priorities in favor of a closer, more intimate relationship with Jesus.

> *Matthew 19:16-22 NLT "Someone came to Jesus with this question: "Teacher, what good deed must I do to have eternal life?"*
>
> *[17] "Why ask me about what is good?" Jesus replied. "There is only One who is good. But to answer your question—if you want to receive eternal life, keep the commandments."*
>
> *[18] "Which ones?" the man asked. And Jesus replied: "You must not murder. You must not commit adultery. You must not steal. You must not testify falsely. [19] Honor your father and mother. Love your neighbor as yourself."*
>
> *[20] "I've obeyed all these commandments," the young man replied. "What else must I do?"*
>
> *[21] Jesus told him, "If you want to be perfect, go and sell all your possessions and give the money to the poor, and you will have treasure in heaven. Then come, follow me."*
>
> *[22] But when the young man heard this, he went away sad, for he had many possessions.*

The rich man believed he was living a holy life by outwardly following the rules. Unbeknownst to him, he was caught up in living for himself and fulfilling his own desires. Many of us live morally upright lives that look good on the outside. People see our actions and may be fooled into thinking we are holy. However, inwardly, we are often striving for more, which blinds us to what the Father is doing around us. This mindset also blocks us from hearing what the Father is asking us to do.

This behavior mirrors that of the Pharisees and Sadducees in the New Testament, whom Jesus frequently criticized. Despite being the holy figures of Israel who meticulously followed the Law, they were blind to God's work around them. Maintaining their grand image and power was more important to the Pharisees than fostering a humble, contrite heart. They prioritized their prestige over simply living for the will of the Father, letting their selfishness obstruct God's glory. Jesus made sure they understood this failure.

To delve deeper, let's examine Matthew 23, which illustrates what a "more" religious life looks like.

Starting with verse 3 (NKJV), Jesus says, *"Therefore whatever they tell you to observe, that observe and do, but do not do according to their works; for they say, and do not do."* Jesus emphasized living a holy life, but never at the expense of glorifying the Father. The Scribes and Pharisees instructed people on how to live outwardly, but their hearts were driven by a desire for more. Verses 5-7 further highlight this hypocrisy: *"But all their works they do to be seen by men. They make their black leather cube shaped cases containing the Torah large and expand the borders of their garments. They love the best places at feasts, the best seats in the synagogues, greetings in the marketplaces, and to be called by men, 'Rabbi, Rabbi.'"*

Understanding these scriptures helps us recognize the importance of focusing on God's will rather than worldly ambitions.

The more life brings us fame and recognition from others, the less Jesus will compete with those distractions. He is a jealous God, and in Matthew 23:8-10, He emphasizes that it's always about Him. Jesus states, *"But you, do not be called 'Rabbi'; for One is your Teacher, the Christ, and you are all brethren. Do not call anyone on earth your father; for One is your Father, He who is in heaven. And do not be called teachers; for One is your Teacher, the Christ."*

As followers of Jesus, we must die to ourselves and daily pick up our cross to follow Him. We need to stop chasing after worldly gains and be content with whatever God desires for our lives. Jesus teaches that true greatness comes from being a servant to all. He understands our desire to be significant, but this significance should be pursued with humility, not pride. In verses 11-12, He states, *"But he who is greatest among you shall be your servant. And whoever exalts himself will be humbled, and he who humbles himself will be exalted."*

This message echoes what Jesus said in Matthew 20:26-28 about how we are to live: *"Yet it shall not be so among you; but whoever desires to become great among you, let him be your servant. And whoever desires to be first among you, let him be your slave—just as the Son of Man did not come to be served, but to serve, and to give His life a ransom for many."*

By embracing humility and serving others, we align ourselves with the true teachings of Jesus and find our true worth in Him.

If we maintain a mindset of always wanting "more," how can we ever truly be a servant to all? This mentality contradicts the very essence of the example Jesus set for His followers. In the world's eyes, greatness is measured by how much one has, but in God's eyes, true greatness is rooted in humility and serving others.

This doesn't mean God cannot bless us with material things. Rather, it means that we should use everything God has given us for His glory and to serve others. To live simply means being content with sitting at the end of the table. If God decides to move us to the front, we are blessed, but seeking that position should never be our main focus.

Luke 14:10 (ESV) says, *"But when you are invited, go and sit in the lowest place, so that when your host comes he may say to you, 'Friend, move up higher.' Then you will be honored in the presence of all who sit at the table with you."*

A "more" mentality will inevitably lead to pride, which will continually obstruct God's work in our lives. While it's true, as Luke 19:40 says, "the rocks will cry out if He needed them to proclaim His glory," God does not require us to accomplish His work; He desires it for us because it's what's best for us.

Matthew 23:13 warns us, *"But woe to you, scribes and Pharisees, hypocrites! For you shut up the kingdom of heaven against men; for you neither go in yourselves, nor do you allow those who are entering to go in."* When we live with a "more" mindset, we risk becoming legalistic. To make ourselves feel better, we might engage in outward displays of righteousness—such as sharing our faith with a coworker or helping the homeless—believing these actions please God. However, these are mere actions unless they stem from a pure and submissive heart to the Lord.

True service to God is not about outward appearances but about aligning our hearts with His will and humbly serving others for His glory.

> Vs 15 says *"Woe to you, scribes and Pharisees, hypocrites! For you travel land and sea to win one proselyte, and when he is won, you make him twice as much a son of hell as yourselves."*

What Jesus is highlighting here is that while we might be doing some good on the surface, our harmful pursuit of "more" will ultimately negatively influence those around us who we are trying to lead to God. According to Jesus, the consequences of this are doubly damaging. We often wonder why so many Christians are leaving the church today. Many have been hurt by other Christians due to extreme condemnation. More mature Christians sometimes adopt a "holier than thou" attitude towards younger believers, condemning them for not doing things the "right" way. Though we might introduce them to Jesus, our lack of understanding of God's grace can eventually push them away.

If we lived simply and understood that our purpose is to glorify the Father in everything we do, we wouldn't try to "fix" others, but rather point them to the Father. A life focused on "more" often brings condemnation to others because it fosters pride within our hearts. Conversely, a simple life emulates Christ, sees others as He sees them, and ultimately leads them to Jesus.

A life rooted in humility and focused on serving God allows us to genuinely support and guide others in their faith journey, rather than pushing them away through judgment and pride.

Today, many people find themselves perpetually busy due to their lifestyle choices. This "more" mentality adds unnecessary complexities to their lives, causing them to make big deals out of insignificant things and never settling for less. Jesus addresses this in Matthew 23:23-24 (MSG):

> *"You're hopeless, you religion scholars and Pharisees! Frauds! You keep meticulous account books, tithing on every nickel and dime you get, but on the meat of God's Law, things like fairness and compassion and commitment—the absolute basics!—you carelessly take it or leave it. Careful bookkeeping is commendable, but the basics are required. Do you have any idea how silly you look, writing a life story that's wrong from start to finish, nitpicking over commas and semicolons?"*

We often focus on what benefits us the most, instead of seeing every situation as an opportunity to bring glory to God. This makes life far more complicated than it needs to be. When we live simply for Jesus,

He takes on the hard work. We simply follow His lead and, most importantly, are content with the results.

By embracing simplicity and focusing on the essentials—fairness, compassion, and commitment—we align ourselves with God's will and find true peace and fulfillment in our lives.

Jesus emphasized the importance of being pure from the inside out, and living a complicated life makes this virtually impossible. In Matthew 23:27-28, He says, *"Woe to you, scribes and Pharisees, hypocrites! For you are like whitewashed tombs which indeed appear beautiful outwardly, but inside are full of dead men's bones and all uncleanness. Even so you also outwardly appear righteous to men, but inside you are full of hypocrisy and lawlessness."*

Jesus is telling the Pharisees that, although they may appear outwardly impressive, their inner lives are filled with corruption and decay. This message can be hard to relate to if we are caught up in a "more" mentality because we often don't recognize that it applies to us. Reflecting on this passage, I began to ask myself some simple questions: If I believe I shouldn't lie, why do I? If I believe I should control my tongue, why do I speak foolishly? If I know I should surrender my circumstances to God and find rest, why am I so anxious and restless?

These questions led me to realize that I was just like the Pharisees. My outward appearance seemed well-rehearsed and proper, but my heart was driven by a desire for more, and it had decayed due to my disobedience. Living simply came as a result of fully surrendering to God; it wasn't initially my main focus. My primary concern was getting ahead, which ultimately led to a life that was decaying from the inside out.

Living simply for Jesus requires an inward transformation, a genuine surrender to God's will. Only then can we be truly free from the hypocritical tendencies that complicate our lives and hinder our relationship with God.

Let's wrap up this chapter by revisiting what we discussed at the beginning. I mentioned that God is fully in control of our lives and that He is directing our paths, even when we may not realize it. Many of us, myself included, have at times lived like the Pharisees, with a controlling, "more" mentality. After reading this chapter, you might recognize areas in your life that need reexamination, especially if living simply has not been your focus.

It's important to remember that no matter where you are in life, God has always been there and will use your life choices up to this point for His Kingdom. When we choose to live simply and surrender to God, He begins to open our eyes to all that He has been doing in and around us. However, for Him to do this, we must relinquish control and be content with the direction He takes us.

Jesus might ask you to confront some difficult areas in your life. He may need to correct parts of your life that aren't best for you. Living simply isn't always easy at first, but as we'll explore in the next chapter, it is ultimately the most rewarding path.

The Art of Contentment: Finding Peace in Simplicity

Talking Points

1. Read Philippians 4:11-13 and answer the following:
   (a)Paraphrase what Paul is saying in your own words and explain what these verses mean to you.

   (b)From where did Paul find the strength to achieve his contentment?

2. Have you ever struggled with a "more" mentality? Explain

3. Was there a time in your life when you were living according to the world's standards, and did you still believe that God was guiding your life? Explain.

4. What does "making things happen" mean in your life?

5. What does it mean to wait on God to initiate things in our lives?

6. How can our material wealth be used for God's glory?

7. What does it mean to you to die to yourself daily?

8. Read Luke 14:7-11 and answer the following:
   (a)Describe this scenario in your own words.

   (b)Why is it important to have a humble spirit?

   (c)Who exalts the humble and why?

9. Read Matthew23:27-28 and answer the following.
   (a)Based on these two verses, describe the Pharisees.

   (b)How should a Christian's heart be conditioned?

10

Simplicity and Fulfillment

Numbers 13:27 NKJV "We went to the land where you sent us. It truly flows with milk and honey, and this is its fruit".

S ome people with driven personalities might say that living simply sounds great for others, but it's not for them. Their lives are structured around a level of complexity that doesn't easily lend itself to simplicity. They are deeply engrossed in what they believe God has blessed them to do, making their lives full of multifaceted responsibilities. For them, the idea of living simply seems impractical, if not impossible, given their numerous commitments and relentless schedules.

Coming from a business background, I resonate with this mindset. My daily duties were incredibly intricate, my time severely constrained, and my to-do list never-ending. Despite this, I remained actively involved in church, participated in Bible studies, tithed regularly, and even went on mission trips. I was convinced I was fulfilling God's purpose for my life—until everything seemed to unravel. My finances and business suddenly plummeted, and nothing went as planned. All I could think about was how to fix the mounting problems.

When we talk about living simply, there are two key perspectives: the physical and the spiritual. The physical aspect encompasses everything we interact with in our daily lives—what we see, smell, touch, and hear—essentially, all that we can control. The spiritual aspect, however, involves perceiving God's work in our lives and ensuring that our life-style reflects His will. Jesus said in John 17, *"we are in the world but not of the world."* This means that while we live in the physical realm, our decisions should be spiritually guided.

When we prioritize God's instructions, our physical lives become inher-ently simpler. Why? Because God directs our path, and the choices we make are for His Glory. Essentially, He takes on the heavy lifting—we just need to follow His lead.

My life was complex, and I rarely made decisions with spiritual guidance as my first priority. When faced with challenges, I didn't surrender them immediately to God; instead, I shifted into "fix it" mode, revealing that I wasn't living simply from a spiritual perspective. Our actions often stem from what we can comprehend, leading us to adjust our physical lives based on what makes the most sense to us. During my past crisis, my focus was more on solving the problem in the physical realm rather than being still and resting in God.

Sure, when opposition arose, I would pray and put on my "spiritual hat," but my primary concern remained on the problem itself—not on seeing the situation through God's eyes. I wasn't thinking about settling for less or finding contentment; instead, I was determined to solve the issue to maintain my lifestyle and status quo. My attitude was that if my back was against the wall, I wouldn't go down without a fight. I would double down, work harder, and eventually pull myself back up. Upon achieving success, I would casually thank the Lord for His blessings and the gifts He had given me, all the while reminding myself that it was His money I was using for His glory.

Deep down, however, my heart wasn't truly aligned with those words. Once I returned to a comfortable life, the next hardship would crash down like a wave. Again, my instinct was to fix it, no matter the cost.

Now, I understand that some of you might not be fighters like me; you might be content with whatever life brings and don't yearn for a grand lifestyle. If that's the case, you're likely further along in understanding the contentment Paul speaks of in his epistles. You might also be closer to grasping how to live a simple spiritual life.

So, I pose this question: How do you handle circumstances? Do you draw nearer to God and see everything happening around you as an opportunity to bring Him glory? Or do you get discouraged, blame others, or seek distractions to cope with your situation?

More importantly, are we honest with ourselves when answering these questions? Are we turning to Jesus first and resting in Him for the long term? It's easy to find short-term relief, but the true test is whether we are willing to journey with Jesus, no matter how long it takes, without succumbing to the pressures of the world.

Addressing problems physically may provide temporary relief, but it often ultimately fails, bringing the issues back with a vengeance. This keeps us trapped in a cycle of highs and lows, preventing us from truly living a simple life. Living simply in the spiritual sense relies on the grace and mercy of our Father. We must rest in Jesus and wait for Him to guide us in what comes next. When I say "rest," I mean a complete rest —of our mind, heart, and thoughts—entrusting everything to God.

Whether we are fighters or peacekeepers, if we do not walk spiritually with simplicity, we may turn to external solutions and fail to trust the one true God. The greatest joy in spiritually living simply is realizing that our problems are not really ours once we surrender them to God. He will handle them. Jesus is the Author and Finisher of our faith, the perfection of all things. He is to be trusted in every aspect of our existence. By walking in the Spirit, we find a life of victory and fewer headaches.

So, how do we achieve this simple life when past methods have failed us? How do we prevent recurring problems from controlling our lives? I want to guide us through the process of living simply both physically and spiritually. We can learn from the Israelites' journey as God led them out of Egypt. The goal is to understand that God has a plan for our lives; He knows what He is doing. He is a good God who wishes to bless us abundantly. Just as He promised the Israelites a land flowing with milk and honey, He wants to bless our lives as well.

Numbers 13:27 (NKJV) says, *"We went to the land where you sent us. It truly flows with milk and honey, and this is its fruit."* To reach this amazing, fruitful, simple life, God will train us to trust Him completely. This will require making significant adjustments in our lives and learning to rest in His ways. Otherwise, reaching the simple life will take longer than we desire, just as it did with the Israelites.

In summary, understanding and embracing simplicity involves a shift in both our physical and spiritual lives. Physically, it means decluttering our environments and schedules; spiritually, it means fully trusting and resting in God's plan for us. By focusing on God's guidance and aligning our actions with His will, we can escape the relentless cycle of temporary fixes and find true, lasting peace and fulfillment.

Just as God led the Israelites to a land overflowing with blessings, He desires to lead us to a life rich with His provisions. Our journey may require patience, trust, and significant changes, but the rewards of living simply in both aspects are more than worth the effort. By surrendering our complexities to Him and embracing His guidance, we can experience an abundant life filled with peace, joy, and divine purpose.

Called Out Of The World

To conquer through surrender by living simply—both physically and spiritually—we must first understand that once we give our lives to Jesus, we must no longer conform to the patterns of this world. The challenge many of us face is that, upon our conversion, we still carry so much of the world's influence that we are often blind to the changes we need to make. Our ingrained habits and ways of dealing with life have led us down paths we thought were best, only to realize, in the face of adversity, that they weren't.

As the Bible says in Psalm 51:5, *"We are born into sin from the moment we were conceived."* The New Living Translation puts it as, "For I was born a sinner—yes, from the moment my mother conceived me." Given this, expecting to have everything figured out immediately after conversion is unrealistic. We cannot live differently without God's help; it's impossible to do it alone. The good news is that Jesus is willing to help us, but it will require change from us. He will take us out of the world we once knew, molding and shaping us into the image He desires. This process will involve unlearning many bad habits and traversing paths that may seem daunting. But there is hope!

In the world, we operate under the illusion that we are in control and that we determine our success. We pursue what we believe is best for us or what pleases others. Naturally, we gravitate toward the things the world offers because that is what we know and understand. We are drawn to the latest fads, tech gadgets, movies, and TV shows. The world offers us comfort in many forms—especially food, like my favorite, dark chocolate (thanks to my wife). These comforts often serve as our go-to soothing agents. While the world gives us many things to help us function and live comfortably, it offers nothing in terms of salvation and hope for eternity.

As mentioned earlier, what the world provides eventually leaves us wanting. Any high you get from worldly things will eventually fade. But with Jesus, your spiritual high is constant and everlasting.

In Exodus chapter 1, the Israelites became enslaved in Egypt because the Egyptians feared their growing numbers and influence. The Egyptians imposed harsh labor on them, showing no mercy. The Israelites suffered greatly, forced to make bricks from mud and perform various other grueling tasks in the fields. Their oppression weighed heavily on them, and they longed for a better life, frequently crying out to God for relief.

As described in Exodus 2:23-25, *"The Israelites groaned in their slavery and cried out, and their cry for help because of their slavery went up to God. God heard their groaning and...looked on the Israelites and was concerned about them."*

It has been suggested that in the Bible, "Egypt" symbolizes "the world," and "Israel" represents "living for God." The Israelites conveyed a message that life in the world was unbearable and they needed divine help. Enslaved and powerless against the daily evils they encountered, they did their best but came to realize there must be a way to achieve freedom. Their attempts to solve their problems within the world proved futile, leading them to reach the end of their efforts and cry out to God. In response, God heard their plea and sent Moses to be His voice to the Israelites.

The Israelites desired freedom but were uncertain about what liberation from worldly bondage would entail. They had to abandon their past, lifestyle, and anything that didn't reflect God's will. They left behind their familiar comforts to follow a God they had only known from a distance. This journey of faith required them to believe in the promise God had given to Abraham of a new and better land. As the Israelites surrendered everything to God, He began to intervene in their situation. Initially, they were skeptical and needed convincing. Understanding this, God sent plagues upon Pharaoh to prove His power, demonstrating His concern not only to Pharaoh but also to the Israelites.

Through these acts, God showed that He was in control, and there was no mistaking His presence and care. As the Israelites witnessed these miracles, they began to see the world with new eyes and gradually started to follow God out of Egypt towards the promised new land.

Living simply in both the physical and spiritual realms requires a deliberate effort to draw closer to God. It involves a mental commitment to follow His guidance for our lives, regardless of the cost. We must be willing to let go of our old lifestyle and place our trust in Him for our new journey. As we do so, we will begin to perceive our circumstances through His perspective.

Life may present us with challenges that seem unfair or hopeless, such as losing a job, facing health issues, or even losing a home. God can use any situation to redirect our focus towards Him. Often, what has the greatest hold over us may become the focal point through which God teaches us to fully rely on Him. In our journey to learn simplicity, He might take us to extremes, removing us from our current situation and leading us into a metaphorical wilderness where worldly distractions are minimized.

Just as Jesus was led by the Holy Spirit into the wilderness for 40 days before beginning His ministry (Matthew 4:1), and Paul spent three years in Arabia to align himself with Jesus' ways (Galatians 1:17), we too may need a period of separation from our familiar surroundings. After spending time in the world, once we are saved, God often intervenes to realign our lives with His perfect will.

My personal experience, as described in the motives chapter, involved a significant teaching process where I had to relinquish my old habits and learn to trust God fully. During my wilderness experience, I faced a choice: to let God provide for my family His way or continue relying on my methods. God made it clear that I was not to intervene. My only commands were to worship Him and wait upon Him. Initially, this approach didn't make sense to me, but God understood that this area had a significant hold on my life. I had to learn to surrender it to Him.

God gave the Israelites a promise to provide them with a land flowing with milk and honey, just as He promised to take care of us when we were saved. Like us, the Israelites had to learn to live according to God's will rather than their own. They needed to accept that they were God's chosen people and that He desired their service. In Exodus 8:1 (NKJV), God instructed Moses to tell Pharaoh, "Thus says the Lord: 'Let My people go, that they may serve Me.'" God doesn't want us to serve ourselves or follow the ways of the world. He wants us to leave all of that behind and serve Him alone.

God has a purpose for every believer's life. He raises each of us to declare His name throughout the earth. As stated in Exodus 9:16 (NKJV), *"But indeed for this purpose I have raised you up, that I may show My power in you, and that My name may be declared in all the earth."* When we are immersed in the world, we lose focus and forget that God is in charge. We unknowingly start living for ourselves and slowly drift away from Him. Exodus 9:29 reminds us, "That you may know that the earth is the Lord's." God is always in control, even when life's circumstances seem chaotic.

The Israelites finally trusted God to lead them to their new life, but not without severe testing. As they were leaving for the wilderness, Pharaoh's army pursued them, threatening to take them back. Exodus 14:10 records, *"The Israelites cried out to the Lord for help."* Despite their initial trust, they struggled to understand why they continued to face problems. They questioned Moses in Exodus 14:11, asking, *"Why would God not allow us to die in Egypt? Why take us to the wilderness to kill us?"* This mirrors our own experiences. Even when our trust is placed in God, challenges arise, tempting us to complain and question His plan. We might think it's easier to return to our old ways.

However, Moses offered crucial advice to the Israelites, which applies to us as well: **BE STILL and know that God is at work**. In Exodus 14:13, Moses reassured them, *"Do not be afraid. Stand still and see the salvation of the Lord, which He will accomplish for you today. For the Egyptians whom you see today, you shall see again no more forever."* God's message to us is the same as it was to the Israelites. Although we still see and fear the world's threats, one day it will no longer have control over us. When challenges arise, we must remember to stand still and trust that God is at work. Even when we face difficulties and uncertainty, His guidance remains steadfast. He calls us to trust in His provision and promises, relinquishing our grip on worldly concerns.

As we journey through life, we may encounter times of testing and temptation to revert to our old ways. Yet, by focusing on God's promises and maintaining our faith, we can overcome these trials. Just as the Israelites experienced God's deliverance, we too will witness His salvation in our lives. By trusting in His sovereignty, we learn to live not for ourselves but for His glory, ultimately fulfilling His purpose for us on earth.

To live simply means to understand that God is for us, and not to misconstrue our circumstances as a result of His displeasure. God is inherently good. As He told the Israelites in Exodus 20:20, *"Do not fear, for God has come to test you, and that His fear may be before you. So that you will not sin."* God's desire is for our lives to be holy, free from sin, as reflected in 1 Peter 1:16, *"Be holy, for I am holy."* He allows our faith and resolve to be tested to help us perceive everything from His perspective.

These trials and challenges teach us to look to Him and let Him work things out. It is when we resist God's testing that we begin to sin. Our impatience and desire to maintain control will lead us to unrest and a longing for the comforts we knew in the past.

The Israelites exemplified this in Numbers 11:4-5, where they constantly complained about the prolonged testing they endured. Verses 4-5 (ESV) state, *"Now the rabble that was among them had a strong craving. And the people of Israel also wept again and said, 'Oh that we had meat to eat! We remember the fish we ate in Egypt that cost nothing, the cucumbers, the melons, the leeks, the onions, and the garlic.'"* They longed for the familiar comforts, forgetting that in Egypt, they were in complete bondage without freedom.

Trusting Jesus to strip our lives of past comforts often leads to temptations and the desire to reclaim them. Satan perpetuates the lie that God is harsh and unloving. In reality, the opposite is true. God loves us so much that He wants us to experience complete joy. He desires for us to live simply, bask in His glory, and reap the fruits of the Father. Satan tries to convince us that God's provisions are insufficient.

The wilderness experience is akin to working out for the first time—initially painful because we are out of shape. Your body feels sore, you're tempted to quit, and you long for the ease of old habits. However, if you persevere, your body begins to feel better and transforms over time. Many avoid working out because it is hard and exhausting. The difference with God is that He is our strength. By drawing near to Him, He provides us with the strength and ability to endure difficulties, shaping us into the people He desires us to be.

> Psalms 28:7 NIV *"The LORD is my strength and my shield; my heart trusts in him, and he helps me. My heart leaps for joy, and with my song I praise him."*

The Israelites were guided by the Shekinah Glory, manifesting as a cloud by day and the appearance of fire by night, as described in Numbers

9:15. This is crucial for us to understand: God leads, and we follow. When He moves, we move; when He is still, we stay still. If we are unsure of His direction, we should remain patient and not act hastily. How do we discern God's leading? By walking closely with Him, we begin to hear His voice more clearly. We start to realize that everything in our lives is about Him, not us. This shift in perspective changes how we view every circumstance and trial. We begin to align our actions with His will, living to please Him and making decisions that glorify Him.

God gave the Israelites a calling—to be set apart so the world would know who He is. He desired them to be holy and to act in ways that reflected His character. He wanted them to shine with His love and treat people as He would. God chose the Israelites as the nation through which salvation would come into the world via His son, Jesus. In the same way, through Jesus, we have been called and set apart. We now have a purpose to emulate Jesus and point others to the Father, just as He did.

As we embrace this calling, our desire for worldly things diminishes because Jesus' love is far greater. We start to live simply, both physically and spiritually. The world's demands on our time become less important, and the priority of living for Jesus takes center stage.

To live simply means to trust Jesus in every aspect of our lives. It involves not depending on what the world offers or relying solely on our understanding. Living simply requires us to move at God's pace, enduring trials without attempting to fix them ourselves and trusting the outcomes to Him. This journey often requires letting go of pride and self-reliance. Our wilderness experience, like that of the Israelites, can be prolonged if we struggle to trust Him. Though their journey to the Promised Land could have taken only 11 days, it stretched to 40 years due to their unwillingness to trust God fully. The journey may be challenging, but the reward of reaching the Promised Land makes it worthwhile.

As stated in Deuteronomy 8:9-11, *"You will lack nothing... when you have eaten and are full, you shall bless the Lord your God for the good land which He has given you. Beware that you do not forget the Lord your God by not keeping His commandments... Remember the Lord your God, for it is He who gives you power to get wealth."*

Once you enter a life of simplicity, everything changes. Your purpose will be renewed and active daily, and your drive for life will become more rewarding and fulfilling. With Jesus in control, all that you do will reflect His incredible love. To God be all the glory, forever and ever. Amen.

Simplicity and Fulfillment

Talking Points

1. Read 1 Peter 1:16 In your own words, describe what it means to be holy.

2. Living Simply: Does living a simple life come naturally to you, or do you find it challenging? Explain your experience.

3. Historical Context: Based on this chapter, outline what happened to the Israelites and the reasons behind those events.

4. Simple Living: What does living simply in both the physical and spiritual sense mean to you?

5. Focus: Problem vs. Jesus: Explain the difference between focusing on your problems and focusing on Jesus.

6. Habits and Simple Living: How do your habits impact your ability to live simply?

7. Read Exodus 20:20 *"Do not fear, for God has come to test you, and that His fear may be before you, so that you will not sin."* Reflect on the following:

   (a)Are you currently fearful of anything in your life? Explain your feelings.

   (b)What does it mean to "fear the Lord," and how can this lead to a life free from sin?

8. Do you have a personal "Exodus" story? Share your experience.

9. In what ways do you feel God is guiding you to live simply today?

11

Long Term Adjustments

2 Corinthians 5:17 NKJV "If anyone is in Christ, he is a new creation, old things have passed away and behold all things have become new."

I love all kinds of sports and have no bias against any of them. Whether it's ping pong or bowling, I'm always up for watching or playing. I guess the appeal lies in the unpredictability of who will win and the thrill of competition. While I enjoy many sports, there are a few that I find particularly entertaining. My favorites include baseball, basketball, golf, and American football.

I know baseball and golf can seem slow to watch and play, but anyone who's ever tried them understands they're far from easy. Both sports have a way of humbling even the most confident players. I recall one round of golf where we experienced this firsthand. The group ahead of us was playing incredibly slowly, and my friends and I grew impatient waiting behind them. Out of curiosity, my friend and I drove our cart down a hill to get a closer look at what was causing the delay.

What we saw was both surprising and hilarious. One of the guys in the group ahead was yelling furiously at his golf bag. To our astonishment, he picked it up and threw it into the pond in a fit of anger. We couldn't help but laugh, along with his buddies, not at him, but because we've all felt the frustration that golf can bring. It's a tough sport, not for the faint-hearted.

The funniest part was yet to come. The guy waded into the pond, and we thought he might have regretted his impulsive act, perhaps due to the cost of the golf clubs. But we were mistaken. He retrieved the bag, took out his car keys and cell phone from the side pockets, and then tossed the bag even further into the center of the pond with renewed determination. My friend and I were cracking up, laughing so hard we could barely speak. We couldn't wait to return to our group up the hill and share the incredible scene we had just witnessed.

I find that sports provide an excellent metaphor for the highs and lows of life. Just as sports take us in various directions, often simultaneously, life demands adaptation and change. To grow, we must constantly adjust to meet life's challenges. Like the frustrated golfer who chooses to react with anger, we can fight against our difficulties, or we can learn to adapt.

Athletes understand the necessity of constant training to excel in their sport. If I were to suggest to an athlete that they don't need to train hard to succeed, they would immediately recognize my lack of understanding. Training is essential for progress and success.

Now, you might think that if you're not athletic or come from a culture where competition isn't emphasized, this metaphor doesn't apply to you. But I encourage you to keep reading. The Apostle Paul frequently used sports metaphors in his teachings as well. For instance, in Philippians 2:12, Paul tells us *"to work out your own salvation with fear and trembling."* While Paul isn't advocating for physical exercise, he emphasizes the importance of putting effort into our relationship with God.

Effort and sports go hand in hand. To live a life that is holy and pleasing to God, we must work at it. The Christian walk is a marathon, requiring discipline and dedication if we are to live in a way that allows God to use us effectively.

> *1 Corinthians 9:24-27 MSG says "You've all been to the stadium and seen the athletes race. Everyone runs; one wins. Run to win. All good athletes train hard. They do it for a gold medal that tarnishes and fades. You're after one that's gold eternally. I don't know about you, but I'm running hard for the finish line. I'm giving it everything I've got. No sloppy living for me! I'm staying alert and in top condition. I'm not going to get caught napping, telling everyone else all about it and then missing out myself."*

Paul understands his calling intimately and is unwaveringly aligned with God's directives. He is focused and determined, embodying a mindset of resilience and readiness for spiritual warfare. Paul's attitude can be summed up as, "Let's gear up and take on Satan's schemes head-on." He knows that discipline is essential; without it, any unexpected challenge could divert him from his path. Paul is acutely aware that Satan's attacks could potentially demoralize him to the point of giving up. Without the proper discipline, he risks being one setback away from total failure.

The four key areas we cover in this book—Trials, Thrive, Live Simply, and Adjust—are intricately woven together. This chapter emphasizes the importance of adjusting our lives to remain constantly within God's will. We will explore the common pitfalls that many of us encounter and, by the end, strive to ignite the same fervor Paul had to live a powerful, Godly life.

A lack of spiritual discipline leaves believers extremely vulnerable to Satan's attacks. As John 10:10 warns, *"The thief comes only to steal and kill and destroy."* It's akin to an athlete being asked to compete in a sport for which they haven't trained or have little experience. The likelihood of failure is high, especially when the competition is elite. Likewise, in our spiritual journey, God calls us to take our faith seriously. If you are a child of God, you are in a spiritual battle and need to be prepared and conditioned for it.

Satan commands an army of demons and strategically seeks to defeat us. In C.S. Lewis's book "The Screwtape Letters," he describes one such tactic, where the devil weaponizes our pleasures against us. A quote from the book illustrates how Lewis portrays Satan's strategy against God's people, whom he refers to as the enemy.

> "Never forget that when we are dealing with any pleasure in its healthy and normal and satisfying form, we are, in a sense, on the Enemy's (God's people) ground. I know we have won many a soul through pleasure. All the same, it is His invention, not ours. He made the pleasures: all our research so far has not enabled us to produce one. All we can do is to encourage the humans to take the pleasures which our Enemy (God's people) has produced, at times, or in ways, or in degrees, which He has forbidden."

This is just one of the many strategies Satan employs against us: using our innocent pleasures for his own gain. However, the more we immerse ourselves in God's word, the stronger we become in recognizing and resisting Satan's attacks. Satan is a fraud who targets our weaknesses. Without walking as disciplined followers of Christ, we risk vulnerability to his destructive blows, which can upend not only our lives but also those connected to us.

We face an elite opponent whose attacks are ruthless, cunning, and relentless, but we are not alone in this battle. As Romans 8:31 reminds us, *"If God is for us, who can be against us?"* With God on our side, and if we lead disciplined lives, Satan has no power over us. Romans 16:20 reassures us further: *"The God of peace will soon crush Satan under your feet.*" Through Christ, we can conquer all challenges, drawing strength from Him.

What does this disciplined life look like? A disciplined life is essential because, without it, we are prone to stumble and fall at every trial we face. Without such discipline, Satan gains the upper hand in many aspects of our lives, causing imbalance and chaos. A follower of Christ must realize that saying yes to God's invitation means surrendering all rights to Jesus. This surrender is the foundation of a disciplined life, and without it, one is mistaken in understanding the true commitment to Christ.

When an athlete commits to becoming the best, he can be in his sport, he must surrender his old ways of competing for new, more effective methods. Similarly, Jesus says in 2 Corinthians 5:17 (NKJV), *"If anyone is in Christ, he is a new creation; old things have passed away, and behold, all things have become new."*

The reason Satan often deceives us and causes us to stumble in difficult times is that we haven't fully embraced this transformation in our minds. For some reason, we still cling to the belief that we retain rights over our own lives. This mindset prevents us from seeing things from God's perspective. Jesus frequently encourages His followers to have eyes that see and ears that hear for this very reason. A true follower of Jesus will cease to view the world through a worldly lens and start seeing it from God's perspective. Without dying to ourselves daily, the circumstances of this world will tear us apart.

> Luke 9:23 reinforces this, stating, *"If anyone wishes to come after Me, he must deny himself, and take up his cross daily, and follow Me."*

It's often said that once you accept Jesus' invitation to follow Him, you join the Lord's army. A popular children's song even goes, "I'm in the Lord's army. Yes, sir!"—and now it's stuck in my head, too. The reality of being in the Lord's army is that we have access to every spiritual weapon imaginable. In Jesus' name, we have the power to move mountains, raise the dead, heal the sick, and walk on water. Our Commander-in-Chief is filled with more love and compassion than anything this world can offer. Moreover, He tells us that through Him, we can possess that same love and compassion. When used for His glory, this love and compassion heap burning coals on the enemy's head.

> *Romans 12:20 ESV "if your enemy is hungry, feed him; if he is thirsty, give him something to drink; for by so doing you will heap burning coals on his head."*

My point is this: living fully in Christ is far more rewarding than anything Satan can offer us.

With that established, let's recognize that we are all at different stages in our walk with Christ, as highlighted in Romans 14. Some of us have walked with the Lord for many years, while others are just beginning and eager to grow. It's crucial to acknowledge that two types of circumstances require us to adjust.

The first type involves life-changing events that permanently alter our direction. These are moments after which we will never go back to our previous ways. The second type includes the everyday challenges we face. If we don't view these daily circumstances from God's perspective, they can derail us and pull us away from Him. This underscores the importance of leading a disciplined life, enabling us to truly see and hear God's guidance.

The level of discomfort you experience as you align your life with God's perfect will depends on your existing habits and spiritual maturity. If you're already disciplined, like an athlete learning a new sport, you'll be more attuned to the training and adjustments ahead. However, if you've been indulging in self-pleasures and neglecting spiritual discipline, you may face painful challenges as you realign your life.

Ultimately, being aligned with Jesus enables us to walk before God in holiness, just as Jesus did during His time on earth.

Let's break down what
Long Term Adjustments Look Like

In life, most people can agree that we go through many seasons and face various circumstances that guide our path and shape who we become. Where we are at 20 years old is likely not where we will be at 50. Life is ever-changing, and in this journey, we can either learn to see change from God's perspective or from the world's perspective. Fully surrendering our lives to Jesus and living a disciplined life is essential for seeing things through God's eyes. Let's now discuss how to allow God to make long-term adjustments when life throws you a curveball without freaking out.

What do I mean by freaking out? Consider these questions regarding circumstances that bring long-term change. How would you respond if your spouse tells you they are having an affair and want a divorce? How would you handle losing your job in a down market? What if you lose a spouse to cancer and your job all in the same year? Or, in a moment of anger, you get into a fight and end up in jail? How do you deal with a failed business or a partner who has cheated you? What if you do not have the money to pay your rent or mortgage and you are forced to move out of your house? Just because these difficult things have happened to us, does that mean God is not good? No! It means God is good and He is right there with you as you adjust your life according to His way. It is up to us to choose whether to allow God to take control in these moments, or to rely on ourselves to find a solution, to repair what is hurting or broken. These defining moments can significantly impact our path and direction for good or for bad.

When faced with these significant events, we experience what Henry Blackaby calls a "crisis of belief" in his book Experiencing God. According to Blackaby, in these moments, God is near and telling us what He wants to do through us. Our response reveals what we believe about God. The word "crisis" comes from a term meaning "decision," signifying a turning point where we must make a choice. Remember, every circumstance is an opportunity for us to bring glory to God. How we respond to major life changes reflects our faith in Jesus.

These moments make us realize that in this world, we will face tribulation and hardship. We will encounter these trials whether or not we have a strong foundation in God. In such moments, we must choose either to surrender to God or to worry and panic. Major events will come, and they will either destroy us or define us in Christ.

So, what is the first thing we should do when faced with these pivotal moments?

Psalms 46:10 "Be still, and know that I am God."

We must understand that as a child of God, He knows of your circumstances and wishes to comfort you.

2 Corinthians 1:3-4 ESV "Blessed be the God and Father of our Lord Jesus Christ, the Father of mercies and God of all comfort, who comforts us in all our affliction, so that we may be able to comfort those who are in any affliction, with the comfort with which we ourselves are comforted by God."

When faced with a crisis of belief, it's crucial to be still right from the start. Without stillness, we can't fully experience the comfort God wants to provide. The next step is to meditate on God's word. Although our flesh may immediately crave answers, the only true answer we need can be found in God's word.

Philippians 4:8 encourages us, saying, *"Finally, brethren, whatever things are true, whatever things are noble, whatever things are just, whatever things are pure, whatever things are lovely, whatever things are of good report, if there is any virtue and if there is anything praiseworthy— meditate on these things."*

Avoid rushing to friends or family for advice or searching the internet for solutions. Instead, stop everything and meditate on God's truth in your life. 2 Corinthians 10:5 reminds us to *"take every thought captive to obey Christ."* Trust that Jesus loves you immensely and that He's in control. Everything is going to be okay. Be still and know that He is God.

After being still for a while and meditating on what is true, you may wonder how to move forward. How do you get on with your life? What's next? The answer lies in what God is telling you! Remember, a disciplined follower of Jesus has eyes to see and ears to hear. In your crisis, Jesus is preparing a path for you to follow. Depending on what He deems best, this period of stillness could be shorter or longer than our patience might desire. Here's where our walk with God often encounters a major challenge.

Long-term adjustments can often occur during periods of calm as well, not just during trials and hardships. Consider instances like falling in love or unexpectedly receiving a job offer in a new location. When these types of long-term changes present themselves, the same principle applies: we need to be still in God's presence and wait for His blessing and direction. What may seem beneficial at first glance may not be what's best for us—it could be driven by our human desires rather than the Spirit's leading. Therefore, it's crucial to seek God's guidance and ensure we hear from Him before making any significant long-term adjustments.

We might understand that God is in control and that meditating on His word is essential, but are we willing to move at God's pace? One of the main reasons we end up in difficult situations is because we act too quickly. Our impatience drives us to "help" God out, prompting us to make decisions we "feel" God wants us to make. We get ahead of God. I often hear people say, "I feel God leading me to do so and so, and by faith, I am going in this direction."

Keep in mind, that God's grace is sufficient, and He can still use us even when we make these hasty decisions. However, that doesn't mean it is His perfect will for our lives. We must learn to trust in His timing and His plans, waiting patiently for His guidance without rushing ahead.

When we study the Bible, we see that God is the one who makes the first move toward us. When God makes Himself known to us, there is no longer an "I feel" moment—it becomes an "I know" moment. There is no mistaking it when God shows up in our lives and invites us to join Him in His work. Consider Moses and the burning bush or Paul on the road to Damascus. Both men had to exercise faith and obedience to what God asked them to do. However, they were not driven by mere feelings; they knew what God was asking of them.

A principle I live by is: "If I don't know, I don't go." I recognize my need for God's guidance and frequently remind Him—and myself—of this. In my discipline of waiting, I dive deeper into God's word. I spend significant time in worship and prayer, honing my focus on His truths and becoming more aware of His work around me. Often, when God makes His presence known, it happens in ways we do not expect. Remember, God does things His way, ensuring that He alone receives the glory.

In Genesis 17, when God told Abraham he would have a child, Abraham was 99 years old, and his wife, Sarah, was 89—well past child-bearing age. God's timing made it clear that it was humanly impossible, thus showing that only He could fulfill such a promise. This teaches us that when we rush ahead and try to "help" God without waiting for His timing, we often end up taking the credit ourselves. It's never about us or what we think is best; it's always about God and His perfect plan. He is a jealous God and desires all the glory, all the time.

Understanding and accepting that God is a jealous God is crucial for our growth during challenging times. If we find ourselves constantly asking "why" and complaining, it likely indicates that we haven't fully surrendered everything to Him. This situation often arises from our own expectations of how we think God should answer our complaints. To align with God's perfect will, we must be willing to go anywhere or do anything He asks of us. Sometimes, God may need to implement drastic changes in our lives to guide us along the path He has set. Resisting His will and clinging to our own will only delay the inevitable and prolong our trials.

The Israelites, for example, spent years on a journey that should have taken days because their murmuring and complaining prevented them from moving forward.

To navigate long-term adjustments and remain in the center of God's will, we must be patient and trust His goodness. God will show up, often in ways we least expect. So, remain steadfast, don't give up, and let God be God.

Remember, just like an athlete training to be the best at their sport, they must undergo changes and long-term adjustments in their lives to achieve their desired results. Similarly, our major trials are opportunities for us to allow God to take ownership of them and guide us toward the best outcomes for us and for His glory.

The main objective of making long-term adjustments is to stay in line with God's perfect will and to find peace that brings joy in upcoming trials. We must never give up and learn to rest in His presence. Though the adjustment might feel never-ending, in the end, it will all be worth it. If you don't resist the direction God is leading you, one day you'll look back and say, "I wouldn't change that time in my life for anything."

In our next chapter, we will focus on how to handle short-term adjustments. While long-term adjustments shape the overall direction of our lives, short-term adjustments are the changes we need to make moment-by-moment decisions to stay aligned with God's work in our daily lives.

LONG TERM ADJUSTMENTS

Talking Points

1. In 2 Corinthians 5:17, what happens when we are in Christ, and what does this mean to you?

2. How do you currently adjust your life when unexpected circumstances arise?

3. As Christians, how are we supposed to adjust our lives when faced with challenging circumstances?

4. How could a life that is not disciplined in Christ affect us physically?

5. How could a life that is not disciplined in Christ affect us spiritually?

6. In 1 Corinthians 9:24-27, Paul references running a race. What is the difference between the perishable crown and the imperishable crown?

(a) What do you think Paul was referring to in verse 27?

(b) To whom was Paul subjecting his body?

(c) What do you think could disqualify him?

7. How can our pleasures leave us vulnerable to Satan's attacks?

8. When faced with difficult circumstances, what should we do first? Explain.

12

Short Term Adjustments

You can't control the wind but you can adjust the Sails. Dolly Parton

Both long-term and short-term adjustments will test our resolve and patience. While long-term patience looks different from short-term patience, both require our steadfastness. Short-term adjustments occur daily, challenging our patience moment by moment as we seek to discern God's presence in each situation. These moments test our faith, requiring us to trust and submit to God's immediate guidance. Conversely, long-term adjustments test our patience over an extended period, demanding endurance and perseverance.

Regardless of the time frame, every decision, thought, and pursuit should aim to glorify God. As Christians, we are called to ensure that our lives reflect God's glory in all that we do. Psalm 86:12 states, *"I will give thanks to You, O Lord my God, with all my heart, and will glorify Your name forever."* This verse highlights our duty to continuously praise and glorify God.

Daily adjustments often challenge us to relinquish our illusion of control and allow God to lead. For example, while writing this chapter, I lost my first draft due to not saving my work. My initial instinct would have been frustration, but instead, I praised God, acknowledging His control over the situation. Missing the save button might have been an accident, but it serves as a reminder of our dependence on God, who directs our paths. When faced with challenges, we frequently perceive them as negative. However, these moments are opportunities to draw nearer to God and place our trust in Him.

The Apostle Paul exemplified a life of constant short-term adjustments. His ministry often placed him in peril, yet he remained motivated to please the Lord and fully aware of God's control. In Acts 14, while preaching in Iconium, Paul faced threats against his life. Despite the dangers, Paul understood that his duty was to follow God's leading, adjusting his actions as necessary. This demonstrates that, like Paul, we must adapt to God's guidance, understanding that our circumstances are part of His greater plan.

> *"Now at Iconium they entered together into the Jewish synagogue and spoke in such a way that a great number of both Jews and Greeks believed. But the unbelieving Jews stirred up the Gentiles and poisoned their minds against the brothers. So they remained for a long time, speaking boldly for the Lord, who bore witness to the word of his grace, granting signs and wonders to be done by their hands. But the people of the city were divided; some sided with the Jews and some with the apostles. When an attempt was made by both Gentiles and Jews, with their rulers, to mistreat them and to stone them, they learned of it and fled to Lystra and Derbe, cities of Lycaonia, and to the surrounding country, and there they continued to preach the gospel." Acts 14:1-7 ESV*

In these seven verses, we see Paul doing what he always did—sharing God's truth with those around him. Paul was deeply convinced that his life should reflect that of Jesus, even to the point of death. Eventually, Paul would be asked to give his life for Jesus, but at this moment, he recognized the changing circumstances around him, prompting him to relocate. Realizing the need for this change, Paul decided to leave Iconium and head to Lystra, where he continued to preach the gospel. His commitment to his mission never wavered; he was always focused on his Father's business.

Studying Paul's life, particularly through his epistles, reveals his understanding that his life was not his own. He knew that whatever he faced each day would be met with the leading of the Holy Spirit. Paul's relationship with the Lord was intimate and genuine, enabling him to see every part of his day as an opportunity to glorify God.

Many people read the Bible thinking it's not relevant to today's world. They assume that things were different back then and that it's hard to relate to Paul, believing his actions were so extraordinary that no modern person could match them. However, Paul's life offers timeless lessons about faith, commitment, and the importance of following God's lead, regardless of the era or circumstances.

To those who doubt the relevance of Paul's example today, I would ask: Do people still need Jesus today? Isn't our world just as perilous now as it was then? Can God not still call someone to love others with the same reckless abandonment that Paul demonstrated? I believe the answer to these questions is a resounding **YES! God desires each of His children to live fearlessly for Him.**

I am writing this chapter on short-term adjustments because many Christians fail to recognize that every moment we live is meant to glorify God. By the time you finish this book, you will have read this statement many times, and I will continue to emphasize its significance. We need to understand that our circumstances and daily decisions are ordained and overseen by God.

> *Psalm 37:23 (ESV) states, "The steps of a man are established by the LORD, when he delights in his way."*

Paul was a man of action. He was content in his calling and pursued God's will regardless of the cost. Paul has given us a clear example of what a driven life for Jesus looks like. He never questioned or complained about God's will or blamed others for his troubles. Instead, Paul constantly adjusted his life and made daily decisions without succumbing to a blame mentality.

Many Christians today tend to blame others or external circumstances for their problems. This blame-shifting diminishes the work God is doing in our lives. The Bible is clear that we are to surrender all to Him and not allow our emotions to lead us astray. Instead of blaming others, we should view every circumstance as an opportunity to see things from God's perspective.

In essence, following Paul's example and embracing God's leadership in every situation enables us to live a life that truly glorifies Him.

Here's a practical scenario that illustrates how we might be tempted to blame others:

Scenario: You recently lost your job and now have no money to pay your electric bill.

Possible Blame:

1. You blame your boss, thinking it was their fault that you were let go.
2. You blame the bad economy, feeling that external economic conditions are responsible.
3. You blame your coworkers, believing their actions contributed to your job loss.

In challenging times like these, it's easy to point fingers and shift blame. However, instead of succumbing to these reactions, we should seek God's perspective and understand that every circumstance is an opportunity to grow in faith and glorify Him. By doing so, we can better navigate life's trials with a heart focused on God's greater plan.

Throughout our lives, we will encounter numerous situations where it might seem easy to blame others. However, what if we considered that these circumstances are no one's fault? Often, we pass the blame as a way to cope with our feelings. But what if we surrendered our need to blame and accepted that God is in control? What if we trusted that He knows exactly what is happening and has allowed these situations for His purposes?

The Bible clearly states that in this world, we will face many tribulations and hardships. By blaming others, we undermine the entire reason Jesus came and lived among us. Jesus came to teach us how to live perfectly by walking in God's will. Because He did so, we can too, with the help of the Holy Spirit. John 16:33 reminds us that *Jesus has overcome the world.* This means that Jesus faced the same hardships we do today. He overcame because He understood that His life was not about Himself but about doing His Father's business.

Jesus saw every situation as an opportunity to bring glory to God, making blaming others pointless. What would be accomplished by blaming others? Would people come to know His Father if He did? Jesus viewed His circumstances as God directing His path. He went with the flow, encountering many who were hurting and in need of healing. Jesus adjusted His life to be in the center of God's will, not for His own sake, but for the sake of others. Had He not viewed His circumstances this way, He wouldn't have been able to be used by God to love others.

As followers of Jesus, we must follow His example and die to ourselves daily. Jesus never blamed others. He adjusted His desires to reflect those of His Father and His mission. If we are to reflect Jesus, we must do the same.

Jesus never worried about money. Why? Because He knew Psalm 50:10: *"For every beast of the forest is mine, the cattle on a thousand hills."* Based on the scenario of losing a job we previously mentioned, and following Jesus' example, we can understand that our circumstances are under God's control. We are called to have eyes to see and ears to hear all that God is doing around us. We can confidently trust that at any moment, God can provide us with the understanding of what He is asking of us. We can also have confidence in knowing that God's word is true and that He will supply all our needs. Jesus never worried about the outcome or blamed others for His difficult situations. He simply adjusted His life to reflect His Father's will, and in doing so, accomplished many wonderful deeds.

In the scripture referenced we read previously regarding Paul, we see that he had to flee to a different city. Yet, this did not stop him from continuing his mission in every new city he entered. When faced with challenging circumstances, as we discuss in the chapter on trials, we should perceive them not as bad but as opportunities for growth. Our trials teach us about the peace of God that surpasses all understanding (Philippians 4:7). Through trials, God opens our eyes to His presence and shows us that He is working everything out for our good (Romans 8:25).

Circumstances and trials are often the moments in your life when you meet new people and witness miracles firsthand. These are times when outcomes unfold without your direct involvement. Perhaps God prompts someone's heart to help you with your electric bill, or a friend unexpectedly recommends you for a job opening. We may not see all the intricate details behind the scenes, but we can trust that God does.

If we choose not to align our lives with what Jesus is doing, we risk falling into a cycle of blaming others and worrying about the outcome. Did you know that Satan gains ground when we succumb to worry? He deliberately cripples us with fear, preventing Jesus from being glorified and causing us to lose in the process.

If God is leading you to submit your resume, do so. Continue to act on the promptings of the Holy Spirit. However, avoid the pitfall of acting solely to feel better or to try to understand everything. Act with the awareness that God is in control, and ensure that all your actions reflect Him and bring Him glory.

"I feel" and "My desires"

Another area of caution, besides blaming others, that Christians need to be aware of is control. Two phrases often misused in this context are "I feel" and "My desire." Many believers use these phrases out of biblical context without even realizing it. If these phrases are not properly aligned with complete surrender to God, they can hinder us when making short-term adjustments.

In contrast, the biblical equivalents would be "I know" and "God's desire." When we say "I feel" in the context of God's leading, we imply that we want God to understand our thoughts and bless our preferred direction, even if we are uncertain. Feelings often lead us to justify actions, seeking validation from others rather than from God. Anytime we need to justify something, it's a clear indicator that it might not be true.

This is not to dismiss genuine emotions. Your feelings are valid—if you feel sick, you might indeed be sick. If you don't feel like going to the mall, then that's simply your current state of mind. However, motives matter. For instance, if you avoid the mall for the wrong reasons, it shows a need for introspection about your heart's intent. In everything we do, we should aim to glorify God.

Sometimes we need to do things we might not feel like doing because God is opening a door. Our lives should be lived with a willingness to adjust to His leading, regardless of our feelings. The truth is, there are times when our bodies genuinely need rest, and it's important to listen to those signals. Resting can be good and necessary, aligning with God's design for us to care for our bodies.

I often hear people say, "My desire is [fill in the blank]." The Bible does state in Psalm 37:4, *"God will give you the desires of your heart."* However, people often overlook the verse preceding it, which says, "Delight yourself in the Lord, and He will give you the desires of your heart." Missing the first part means missing the context for the promise. Without this context, people may misunderstand what desires God is actually talking about.

For example, I often hear people say, "If God gives me more money, I will use it for His good." However, an examination of their current financial stewardship often reveals they are not using the little they have for good purposes. They mistakenly think that because God is loving, He will automatically bless their desires, which are rooted in their personal feelings rather than in alignment with God's will.

This can go either way. If our desire genuinely aligns with God's desire and brings Him glory, then God may indeed grant us the resources we seek. However, if our desires do not reflect His perfect will for us, we risk misapplying God's truth for personal gain. Therefore, it is crucial to ensure that our desires are rooted in delighting in the Lord and seeking to glorify Him in all that we pursue.

> *Matthew 16:23 ESV "Jesus said to Peter "Get behind me, Satan! You are a hindrance to me. For you are not setting your mind on the things of God, but on the things of man."*

Our culture and societal influences often shape our perspectives to align with worldly values. If we are not vigilant, the pursuit of what the world offers can easily lead us away from God and significantly hinder our spiritual awareness.

> *2 Corinthians 4:18 NIV "So we fix our eyes not on what is seen, but on what is unseen, since what is seen is temporary, but what is unseen is eternal."*

As discussed in the last chapter, "Long Term Adjustments," there's an important distinction between feeling or thinking about what God wants for our life and truly knowing it. With short-term adjustments, we constantly make daily decisions that may not conclusively tell us if they will bring glory to God. This approach encourages us to move away from phrases like "I feel" and "my desire," and embrace "knowing God's will" and "desiring all that God desires."

Paul exemplified this in Acts 20:22 when he expressed to the Ephesian elders that he was compelled by the Spirit to go to Jerusalem. Despite not knowing what awaited him, Paul was certain that the Spirit was leading him, even if it meant facing possible death. Not once did Paul say, "It feels like" God is leading him, nor did he express personal desires to return to Jerusalem. His focus was not on his own desires but on ensuring that God was glorified.

We must tread carefully with statements like "I feel" and "I desire." If these sentiments are not aligned with God's broader plan for our lives, they can be manipulated by Satan.

Reflecting on Paul, it's clear he was intense in his dedication, urging his followers to adopt the same steadfastness. In 1 Corinthians 11:1, Paul instructs, "Follow my example, as I follow the example of Christ." As emphasized in the previous chapter, being disciplined in our walk with

Christ and viewing life from God's perspective, rather than our own, is crucial.

This is especially true if we aim to make daily decisions that best reflect God's perfect will in our lives. Paul exemplified this discipline by living a life committed to knowing and doing the will of God.

In 1 Corinthians 9:27, Paul states, *"But I discipline my body and keep it under control, lest after preaching to others I myself should be disqualified."* A disciplined life should reflect Jesus in every decision we make, every action we take, every thought we think, and even in our spoken words. We've all heard the phrase, "What Would Jesus Do?" Although simple, this statement holds profound truth. It's not about acting this way just when we feel like it; it's a lifestyle commitment. Our motives and habits play a significant role in shaping this lifestyle.

Many of us are tempted to base decisions on feelings and desires due to deeply embedded bad habits. Addictions, for example, are habits that create a false reality, diverting us from depending on God. There are also habitual behaviors designed to control or manipulate situations to reflect our interests.

Consider how you react when someone cuts you off on the freeway—do you immediately feel the urge to retaliate? Or when someone opposes your ideas or leadership style—are you tempted to correct them forcefully or lose your temper? How do you feel when a coworker, who may not be as competent, is your boss? Do you often find yourself critiquing others, easily pointing out their faults without considering that perhaps you share those very flaws?

Examining and changing these habitual responses is crucial for aligning our day-to-day decisions with God's perfect will. By doing so, we cultivate a disciplined life that consistently seeks to reflect Christ in every aspect.

These kinds of habits are rooted in sin. We engage in them to elevate ourselves as superior while diminishing the value of the person we're dealing with. The Bible says in Philippians 2:3, *"Do nothing from selfish ambition or conceit, but in humility count others more significant than yourselves."* If we lose perspective and start viewing circumstances or people as threats, we fail to see them as Jesus does. John the Baptist understood that to live a surrendered life, our self must decrease so that Jesus can increase. God did not create us to control people or circumstances; He wants us to recognize situations from His perspective and obediently adjust our lives accordingly.

We must relinquish the notion that life is about us. As children of God, our lives are always about Him. If someone cuts you off on the freeway, your response should be to pray for that person. If your boss lacks your knowledge, you should elevate them higher than yourself and do whatever it takes to make them look better. It's never about you; it's about Jesus being glorified in and through everything you do.

The old Christian saying "Garbage in, Garbage out" rings true here. If we fill ourselves with worldly things, then the world will come out of us. Conversely, if we fill ourselves with God, His character will manifest through us. Consuming our lives with garbage leads to bad habits, which distract us from Jesus and focus attention on ourselves. Consequently, our feelings and desires will align with what we want rather than what God wants for us. This is a significant issue when making short-term adjustments to discern God's will versus what we "feel" His will is. It's also problematic when our lives are so consumed with worldly things that our habits lead us to desire what the world offers instead of what God desires for us.

For a follower of Jesus to walk in holiness in their daily life, they must recognize the necessity of making adjustments. These adjustments need to be made with the proper perspective, ensuring that everything they do is aimed at bringing glory to God, not themselves. There is an enemy intent on distracting us from making forward progress. Learning to see daily obstacles and circumstances from God's point of view helps us defeat Satan and enables us to thrive in the moment.

I pray that we walk with great power in the Holy Spirit and that God's great grace shines on us all. Acts 4:33 (NKJV) states, *"With great power the apostles gave witness to the resurrection of the Lord Jesus, and great grace was upon them all."* If we learn to view every circumstance from God's perspective and adjust our lives accordingly, we will gain the power to overcome every trial that comes our way.

Now that we understand the importance of both long-term and short-term adjustments for true spiritual growth, in the next chapter, we will explore how to thrive in every moment regardless of our circumstances.

SHORT TERM ADJUSTMENTS
Talking Points

1. What is the difference between long-term adjustments and short-term adjustments?

2. How do you initially react when circumstances arise? Explain.

3. Read Psalm 37:23 and paraphrase it in your own words.

4. Give some examples of how you can view every part of your day from God's perspective. Explain.

5. Have you ever found yourself blaming others when circumstances arise? Explain.

6. Read John 16:31-33 in The Message version and answer:
   (a) Who abandons Jesus and why?

(b) Who is with Jesus?

(c) What did He tell the disciples would happen?

(d) What happens when we trust Jesus?

7. Do you see your life as being "about the Father's business?" Why or why not?

8. What is the difference between the "I feel God is saying" mentality and the "I know God is saying" mentality?

9. What is the difference between the "my desire(s)" mentality and the "God's desire" mentality?

10. Read Psalm 37:3-8 and answer the following:
   (a) What is the Lord asking you to do?

(b) According to these verses, what happens when we submit to the Lord?

(c) What happens when we fret or are angry?

11. Explain how having more of the world in us will hinder us from making adjustments for God's glory.

13

Thrive in Your Moment- Part 1

So Jesus explained himself at length. "I'm telling you this straight. The Son can't independently do a thing, only what he sees the Father doing. What the Father does, the Son does. The Father loves the Son and includes him in everything he is doing. (John 5:19-20 MSG)

I once heard that high achievers quickly identify rich opportunities, make swift decisions, and leap into action immediately. Today, numerous motivational books and quotes inspire us to keep pushing forward. Nike encapsulates this spirit with their slogan "Carpe Diem," meaning "seize the day" or "excel in your moment." To become a high achiever, it undeniably requires discipline, hard work, and a keen sense of seizing every opportunity that comes your way.

High achievers are those who succeed consistently or are highly determined to succeed at all costs, often embodying a 'never give up' attitude. Their mantra could be something like, "Nothing happens unless you make it happen." These individuals constantly keep their foot on the pedal, always ready to move. However, not all high achievers are aggressively pursuing every opportunity. Some are content excelling in their domain, leveraging their unique talents and skills, and taking advantage of opportunities when it feels right and safe. On the other hand, some people are perfectly fine with doing their jobs, earning a paycheck, and living securely and with less risk.

American culture today promotes the idea that we live in the land of the free, where hard work and determination can help us achieve anything. We often hear that with a little effort and discipline, anything is possible. But what happens when circumstances change? What about individuals who have worked tirelessly, only to see their dreams shattered by a tragic accident? Or those who dread competition and struggle when they must compete to advance in their careers? These individuals may find themselves underperforming and feeling defeated because they weren't willing to do what their competitors did to get ahead.

Yes, hard work can lead to success, but how far are we willing to go? Are we willing to hurt others in our quest to achieve our dreams? Do we invest so much in our careers that we lose sight of why we started working in the first place? We often hold great expectations for the future, but when life throws us curveballs, it can utterly crush our dreams, leaving us feeling hopeless and drained.

Whether you're a high achiever or someone who simply aims to get by, God desires all of us to succeed at a high level according to His will and way. He has great plans for our lives, as Jeremiah 29:11 (ESV) states: *"For I know the plans I have for you, declares the Lord, plans for welfare and not for evil, to give you a future and a hope."* The world can offer us temporary rewards like money, fame, and a sense of self-worth based on our endless efforts. In contrast, God offers us an abundant life grounded in our relationship with Him, based on His unfailing love. While worldly success may eventually lead to despair and heartache, success according to God's way leads to rejoicing and an abundant life, as stated in John 10:10.

Jesus's way is not for the lazy; it requires sacrifice and commitment. He calls us to lay down our lives for the sake of others, demanding constant obedience and hard work in everything we do. The key difference is that our hard work is not for our boss or ourselves, but for God's Kingdom. As Colossians 3:23 (NIV) says, *"Whatever you do, work at it with all your heart, as working for the Lord, not for human masters."* Human effort in the physical realm produces fleeting moments of happiness, whereas human effort in the spiritual realm produces a lifetime of joy.

What Does Working for The Lord Mean?

Working for the Lord means being content in the job God has given us. We seek our careers with God's guidance and rest in the direction He leads us. This perspective transforms how we view our work; we see everything we do as unto Him and remain willing to adjust our lives at any given moment to glorify Him. Each day becomes an opportunity to thrive in the moment He has provided.

A follower of Christ measures success differently than how our culture has taught us. For believers, success isn't defined by a paycheck or influence. Instead, success means doing the will of our Heavenly Father, glorifying Him through our work no matter what it is. As Galatians 5:13 (NIV) states, *"You, my brothers and sisters, were called to be free. But do not use your freedom to indulge the flesh; rather, serve one another humbly in love."* We don't seek careers to satisfy ourselves or to be deemed accomplished by our peers. We pursue our vocations so that we may use our gifts in a way that attracts others to Christ.

> Hebrews 6:10 (NIV) reassures us, *"God is not unjust; He will not forget your work and the love you have shown Him as you have helped His people and continue to help them."*

Success according to Jesus means thriving in every moment God gives us. It involves viewing our job or career through Jesus' eyes, seeing each moment as an opportunity to represent Him. True success is being trusted by the Father to be included in all that He is doing.

John 5:19-20 MSG "So Jesus explained himself at length. "I'm telling you this straight. The Son can't independently do a thing, only what he sees the Father doing. What the Father does, the Son does. The Father loves the Son and includes him in everything he is doing."

That phrase Nike uses "Carpe Diem", to seize the day would apply to our spiritual life as well. The Bible shows us that Jesus was always about His Father's business. He was always looking for what His Father was already doing. Jesus understood that He was on this earth to thrive in every moment that God entrusted Him with. He told His disciples multiple times to have eyes to see and ears to hear because He knew that His Father was always working and speaking. Our calling is very much like Jesus' calling. We are here to point people to the Father for salvation. Granted He was perfect and had to die for everyone, which is something none of us can measure up to. However, we can be available to others, not by beating them over the head with our Bibles, but by loving them in areas that our Father reveals to us at that moment.

How Do We Love Others to Christ?

Achieving success is quite straightforward: it involves using the gifts and talents that God has graciously given us. While this understanding is widely accepted, it is not often put into practice. Although we know we can lead others to Christ through love, we frequently fail to recognize our Father at work around us. We miss these opportunities for various reasons, often due to misaligned motives that cause us to live for fleshly desires.

Consider this example: a friend asks you to meet them at a bar after work. If your motives are pure, there should be no issue with going to the bar. However, if your motives are not pure and being at the bar could lead you into drunkenness, lust, envy, or other temptations, should you still go? Or would it be wiser to meet somewhere else?

1 Corinthians 6:12 (ESV) states, "All things are lawful for me, but not all things are helpful. All things are lawful for me, but I will not be dominated by anything."

To thrive in our moment, we must ask ourselves, "Am I engaging in this activity for God's glory or for my benefit?" Each of us is different, so we need to honestly evaluate whether our actions are profitable for God's glory. Jesus associated with drunks (not implying your friend is one) and loved them, but He did so in a way that did not cause Him to stumble. Similarly, we must put ourselves in positions to thrive, not to falter.

A follower of Jesus must take his calling seriously and be obedient when the Father reveals Himself. Otherwise, the gifts and talents God has given us may be taken away and given to someone else.

Let's read the Parable of the Talents in Mathew 25 to underscore what I mean.

"For it will be like a man going on a journey, who called his servants and entrusted to them his property. To one he gave five talents, to another two, to another one, to each according to his ability. Then he went away. He who had received the five talents went at once and traded with them, and he made five talents more. So also he who had the two talents made two talents more. But he who had received the one talent went and dug in the ground and hid his master's money. Now after a long time, the master of those servants came and settled accounts with them.

And he who had received the five talents came forward, bringing five talents more, saying, 'Master, you delivered to me five talents; here, I have made five talents more.' His master said to him, 'Well done, good and faithful servant. You have been faithful over a little; I will set you over much. Enter into the joy of your master.' And he also who had the two talents came forward, saying, 'Master, you delivered to me two talents; here, I have made two talents more.' His master said to him, 'Well done, good and faithful servant. You have been faithful over a little; I will set you over much. Enter into the joy of your master.'

He also who had received the one talent came forward, saying, 'Master, I knew you to be a hard man, reaping where you did not sow, and gathering where you scattered no seed, so I was afraid, and I went and hid your talent in the ground. Here, you have what is yours.' But his master answered him, 'You wicked and slothful servant! You knew that I reap where I have not sown and gather where I scattered no seed? Then you ought to have invested my money with the bankers, and at my coming, I should have received what was my own with interest. So take the talent from him and give it to him who has the ten talents.

For to everyone who has will more be given, and he will have an abundance. But from the one who has not, even what he has will be taken away. And cast the worthless servant into the outer darkness. In that place there will be weeping and gnashing of teeth."
Mathew 25: 14-30

I included this parable to emphasize that God desires us to be faithful with the talents and gifts He has entrusted us with. If God has given you five talents, He expects you to use them diligently. Obediently using our talents means that, over time, God will entrust us with more. Conversely, if we neglect to use our talents when He calls upon us, He will take them away and give them to someone who will utilize them. God has given each of us with talents and gifts to help us thrive in our Christian walk and achieve success His way.

Jesus exemplified perfection because He possessed all gifts and talents—a completeness that most of us do not have. However, Jesus gives us specific gifts and talents tailored to our success in His work. We must be content with what He has given us and remain aware of His work around us. Jesus positions us for success when we use our natural abilities to bring Him glory. For example, if we have the gift of teaching, and it comes naturally to us, God will use that gift for His Kingdom, leading us to places or people who need to be taught His truths. Similarly, if we have the gift of hospitality, we will naturally invite people into our lives to bless them.

One universal gift we all share is the ability to love and tell others how Jesus has changed our lives. Every believer has been given this gift, yet it is often the least utilized. Jesus commanded His followers in Mark 16:15 to share His truths: "Go into all the world and proclaim the gospel to the whole creation." There are many people in our lives who need to hear about God's great love. It is our duty as followers of Jesus to seize these moments whenever God opens doors for us to share His truths.

Beyond selfish reasons, another obstacle to sharing God's love is our reluctance to step out of our comfort zones. Many of us live like hermits, confined within our shells and unwilling to engage with others. If we are serious about being obedient to Jesus by using our gifts, we must make ourselves available to people. Jesus was in the business of serving and loving people, and our lives should mirror that commitment.

If fear is preventing you from sharing God's truth with others, remember 2 Timothy 1:7: *"For God has not given us a spirit of fear, but of power and of love and of a sound mind."* Jesus assures us that He will provide the words to say, eliminating any need to worry. As Mathew 10:19 states, *"Do not be anxious about how you are to speak or what you are to say, for what you are to say will be given to you in that hour."*

There are few valid excuses, apart from possibly medical reasons, for not engaging in our Father's work. Keep in mind, *"greater is He who is in you than he who is in the world"* (1 John 4:4). As God's children, we should seize every opportunity He presents to share His truth. I assure you, it is God's will, and He will provide us with continual opportunities.

If we fail to use our gifts for His glory, how can He trust us with greater responsibilities in His Kingdom? It is crucial to recognize the importance of being obedient and utilizing the gifts and talents that God has given to us.

Stephen's Faith

Stephen, the disciple in Acts chapters 6 and 7, exemplifies what it means to thrive in one's moment. Despite the challenges he faced, Stephen likely experienced fear at times, much like many of us do when stepping out in faith. He lived in a culture hostile to Jesus, similar to the world we find ourselves in today. At some point in his conversion experience, Stephen had to reconcile his faith in Jesus. He needed to either fully trust in everything Jesus said about Himself or become a nominal, 'closet' Christian. This was Stephen's journey of working out his salvation.

> *Philippians 2:12 (NKJV) encourages us, "Therefore, my beloved, as you have always obeyed, not only as in my presence but much more in my absence, work out your own salvation with fear and trembling."*

Acts 6:3 tells us that Stephen had a good reputation, was full of the Holy Spirit, and possessed Godly wisdom. These attributes demonstrated that Stephen walked closely with Jesus and reflected His characteristics. Acts 6:8 (NKJV) further illustrates Stephen's faith and power: *"And Stephen, full of faith and power, did great wonders and signs among the people."* Stephen's faith was not just theoretical; it was backed by action. He stepped out in faith and became a warrior for Jesus.

To thrive in our moment requires a commitment to walking closely with Jesus. Though it can be challenging, the outcome is transformative. Stephen received spiritual power, akin to the kind described in Romans 16:20: *"to crush Satan beneath our feet."* His gifts and talents resulted in great wonders and signs among the people. Had Stephen not been trustworthy in using his gifts for God's glory, he might have lost them. Followers of Christ need to understand that Stephen was an ordinary man just like us. Before knowing Jesus, he was simply a servant waiting on tables. The difference came through his intimacy with the Father, which empowered him profoundly.

This intimacy gave Stephen boldness and the ability to perceive everything the Father was doing. By consistently thriving with our gifts and God's power, we too become instruments of significant impact. We become spiritual warriors, dismantling Satan's power and glorifying Jesus in every moment.

I often use the term "we become weapons of mass destruction" because God's power profoundly influences outcomes. A warrior on fire for Jesus wields immense power when combating Satan's attacks. Along with this power comes great knowledge and wisdom, far beyond what one could attain living for oneself. When this potent combination is aligned with God's will, it creates a "shock and awe" effect against the enemy. The world stands in amazement when this divine power is unleashed. People cannot comprehend the pure love, gentleness, long-suffering, and peace that believers exhibit, especially in trials. They recognize that you are not of this world and will either oppose you or join God's kingdom. However, if we fail to thrive in our moments, the world loses its chance to choose. Jesus uses these opportunities to build His church, choosing us to seize every moment He provides.

Take Stephen, for example. In Acts chapters 6 and 7, we see a prime example of what it means to thrive in one's moment. I don't know exactly what Stephen was doing when people started attacking him verbally, but Acts 6:10 makes it clear that his power was on full display. He was thriving in that moment: *"And they were not able to resist the wisdom and the Spirit by which he spoke."* His great wisdom left his attackers unable to counter him. When they couldn't defeat him fairly, they resorted to false accusations and rallied others against him.

Thriving in our moments may or may not provoke such a reaction from people. However, if a significant stir arises as it did with Stephen, we can be sure God has a plan. Our task is to trust in Jesus, not in our circumstances, and continue thriving.

It is always beneficial to see the outcomes of our struggles in advance, but Stephen did not have this privilege. The people managed to persuade enough others to believe their lies against Stephen, leading to his appearance before the council. Imagine being in his shoes, dragged to court to defend your faith before corrupt judges. Would you view this situation from a worldly perspective, fearing that your life was over? Or would you adopt God's perspective, seeing it as an opportunity to thrive despite the challenges?

Stephen chose to see it as an opportunity to glorify his Savior. He understood that he was called for such a time as this and believed that the outcomes were already determined by God's plan. His role was to faithfully execute what God was asking of him.

Filled with the Holy Spirit and immersed in God's boundless love, Stephen opened his mouth before these men, and God provided him with a sermon unlike any other. He delivered it with a boldness that only comes from above. Stephen skillfully connected the Old Testament with the New Testament, giving the council a chance to come to Jesus. Despite their reaction—gnashing their teeth and becoming infuriated —Stephen remained unshaken and steadfast.

Let's read Acts 7:54-60 and see the end of this amazing story.

> "Now when they heard these things they were enraged, and they ground their teeth at him. ⁵⁵ But he, full of the Holy Spirit, gazed into heaven and saw the glory of God, and Jesus standing at the right hand of God. ⁵⁶ And he said, "Behold, I see the heavens opened, and the Son of Man standing at the right hand of God." ⁵⁷ But they cried out with a loud voice and stopped their ears and rushed together[a] at him. ⁵⁸ Then they cast him out of the city and stoned him. And the witnesses laid down their garments at the feet of a young man named Saul. ⁵⁹ And as they were stoning Stephen, he called out, "Lord Jesus, receive my spirit." ⁶⁰ And falling to his knees he cried out with a loud voice, "Lord, do not hold this sin against them." And when he had said this, he fell asleep."

Stephen's life stands as a testament to a man who understood that his existence was not about himself, but wholly about his Father. When reading this book, if we don't grasp that our lives should reflect what we see our Father doing, we have missed its fundamental message. Stephen embraced his calling with the utmost seriousness and was willing to die so that God's Son would be glorified. He did not fear the consequences of living a life fully dedicated to Jesus and remained steadfast in every moment God gave him, despite his circumstances.

Notice in verse 58, the mention of Saul's name. It's no coincidence that Luke, the author of Acts, included this detail. Saul, who later became the Apostle Paul, was present at Stephen's execution, witnessing the events unfold firsthand. I believe this was a pivotal moment that God used to open Paul's eyes to what a true servant of God looks like. Once converted, Paul could draw from this powerful experience, embodying the same boldness Stephen displayed.

Who knows if Paul would have come to faith without Stephen's testimony? Our role is not to control the results but to be obedient to what

God calls us to do. We can trust that God works all things together for good (Romans 8:28). Our responsibility is to follow God's plans in His way, adjust our lives to His actions, and thrive in every moment He grants us. In our next chapter, we will continue our conversation on thriving in our moments.

THRIVE IN YOUR MOMENT – PART 1
Talking Points

1. Colossians 3:23 NIV: "Whatever you do, work at it with all your heart, as working for the Lord, not for human masters." In your own words, explain the meaning of this verse. How do you feel called to live it out in your daily life?

2. Do you view your life primarily from your own desires and ambitions, or from the perspective of what God wants for you? Explain your stance.

3. When you work hard, is it mainly to please others, or to glorify God through your efforts? Reflect on your motivations.

4. In what ways have you tried to attain success according to your own will? Provide examples.

5. What has success looked like in your life up to this point? Share your experiences and insights.

6. Explain how success, according to Jesus, involves thriving in every moment for God's glory.

7. Parable of the Talents: Read Matthew 25:14-30 and answer the following questions.
   (a) What did the servant with 5 talents do, and what was the result?

   (b) What did the servant with 2 talents do, and what was the result?

   (c) What did the servant with 1 talent do, and what was the result?

   (d) What do you think the talents in this parable symbolize? Explain your reasoning.

   (e) What spiritual principles are taught through this parable?

8. Learning from Stephen: Acts 6 & 7 How did Stephen thrive in his final moments, and what lessons can we draw from his example for our own lives?

14

Thrive in Your Moment - Part 2

"I used to ask God to help me. Then I asked if I might help Him. I ended up by asking God to do His work though me."
– Hudson Taylor

"He said, "Love...as I have loved you." We cannot love too much."
- Amy Carmichael

Paul - the determined Warrior for Jesus

Let's take a closer look at the Apostle Paul's life. As a determined and committed individual, Paul took his role very seriously. When he was a Pharisee, he carried out his duties with relentless precision, driven by a personal vendetta against Christ's followers, and filled with pure hatred towards them. This all changed dramatically when he encountered Jesus on the road to Damascus. That pivotal moment transformed Paul's life entirely.

Paul had what many refer to as a "come to Jesus" moment, where his eyes were opened wide to God's truth. According to Acts 9:20, immediately after his conversion, Paul began preaching in the synagogues that Jesus is the Son of God. His conversion was extraordinary and highlighted by his encounter with Jesus Himself.

Unlike most conversions, which may have unique and inspiring stories, Paul's was marked by a direct meeting with Christ. Promptly after his conversion, Paul was compelled to share God's truth with others. Although he took time to retreat to Arabia for three years to unlearn his old ways, he understood his duty as a follower of Christ: to proclaim the message of Jesus.

Whenever we choose to love others and view life from God's perspective, it demonstrates our desire to thrive in our moment. We will undoubtedly face unforeseen circumstances that test our faith deeply, challenging us with situations that might seem unfair and shake our spiritual foundations. In these critical moments, we have a choice: to rise and act according to Jesus' teachings or to fall short.

While it's true that we all fall short at times, this does not disqualify us from striving to give God our very best, prioritized effort. Each day we are given is another opportunity to put on the full armor of God and prepare for the battles we face. God desires us to succeed daily by seeing every moment as an opportunity to thrive as Jesus would.

Paul's epistles highlight his extraordinary success in spreading the gospel of Jesus. His ministry, along with the work of other apostles, significantly impacted the world, turning it upside down. However, this success did not come without facing immense opposition and persecution. Paul was a dedicated warrior for God who put on the Full Armor of God daily. He wielded the sword of the Spirit to combat evil and frequently relied on the shield of faith as he encountered relentless attacks in nearly every city he visited. His life was a constant whirlwind of spiritual battles, where he was often casting out demons, healing the sick, saving the lost, or enduring beatings and imprisonment. There was never a dull moment for Paul; he was always on call and ready to achieve victories for Jesus.

For Paul to achieve such victories, he had to understand that God was in control of every moment of his life. He knew that his life was meant to be a beacon of light, reflecting Jesus in everything he did. If Paul had not taken his role seriously and viewed his calling from this perspective, he would never have recognized God's work in his life and would not have thrived for Jesus when it mattered most.

It is imperative that we grasp this concept and ask ourselves two crucial questions: **"Are we warriors for Jesus?"** and **"Are we, like Paul, willing to thrive in our moment for His glory?"**

Don't let Satan convince you that you are different from Paul, that you are not called to ministry like he was, or that you cannot do what Paul did. These are lies meant to discourage you. God calls each of us to die to ourselves daily and follow Him. He desires us all to embrace our roles as His servants, just as Paul did, and to fulfill His will in every moment we are given.

You must believe this if you are to overcome the hang-ups and past hurts that have been holding you back. Trials are opportunities to thrive, but if you don't truly believe that you are called to be like Paul or any of the apostles, you will struggle to overcome these challenges and will fall victim to them instead.

By understanding and embracing your calling, you can tap into the strength and guidance that God provides. Remember, every trial is an opportunity to grow and demonstrate your faith. Just as Paul faced immense challenges and opposition, yet thrived through his unwavering commitment to God, you too can overcome and thrive in your faith journey. Believe in your calling, trust in God's plan, and face each challenge with the confidence that you are equipped and called to serve Him victoriously.

Let's consider a few instances in Paul's life where he had the opportunity to either grumble in defeat or rise up and thrive. In Acts 16:16-40, Paul was in Philippi with a single-minded focus: to share the Gospel of Jesus with the people there. During his journey, he encountered a slave girl with psychic abilities who followed him everywhere, proclaiming to everyone that Paul and Silas were servants of the Most High God. Despite this potential distraction, Paul remained steadfast in his mission, highlighting his determination and unwavering commitment to his calling.

Through these experiences, Paul exemplifies the importance of recognizing God's hand in every situation and responding with faith and resilience. Like Paul, we too must be prepared to thrive in our moment, embracing our role as warriors for Jesus and seeking to bring glory to God in all that we do.

As I read Acts 16:16-40, I asked myself, what options did Paul have in this moment? How would I respond to someone who was annoying me or interfering with my ministry? My initial thought was that if Paul saw the girl the way the world saw her, he would have definitely been bothered. But, what if he saw her the way Jesus would have seen her? He would have had great compassion for her, rather than being annoyed.

My next thought was that demons recognize true servants of the Most High God. If I were in the same situation as Paul, could I find comfort in knowing that I am a child of God? As it says in Acts 19:15, *"And the evil spirit answered and said, Jesus I know, and Paul I know; but who are you?"* It would be both a privilege and a formidable thought to be known by Satan and to know he is concerned about my impact for God's Kingdom. This can be daunting, but I trust that if God is for me, nothing can stand against me.

Returning to the original question: what options did Paul have? He could have told the girl to shut up and reported her to the authorities for harassment. Personally, knowing my tendencies, I might have chosen this option. He could have tried to avoid her by dodging through the crowd. Or, he could have seized the moment to glorify God.

This realization brings me to one final thought: what was the most important thing this slave girl needed? She needed to be set free and saved for eternity.

So, what did Paul do? As we read in Acts 16:18 (ESV): *"Paul, having become greatly annoyed, turned and said to the spirit, 'I command you in the name of Jesus Christ to come out of her.' And it came out that very hour."* I love how honest the Bible is in depicting Paul's annoyance. I am grateful that Luke, the author of Acts, included that detail because it makes Paul relatable. Despite his annoyance, Paul handled the situation in the spirit.

When facing opposition, the Bible reminds us that our battle is not against flesh and blood but against underlying spiritual darkness. To win for Jesus and thrive in our moments, we must fight our battles in the spirit, not in the flesh. In the flesh, we will always lose and let Satan gain ground, but when we battle in the spirit, we will always win, and Jesus is glorified. Thanks to Paul's example, we now understand that even if we are annoyed by the trials and tribulations we face, we can find strength and perseverance through our faith. Paul teaches us that our struggles can serve a greater purpose when we remain rooted in God's power and love. By keeping our focus on the spiritual battle and trusting in the Holy Spirit, we can overcome any challenge and reflect Christ's victory.

As we move further into the story, we learn that Paul unleashed a hornet's nest of demonic warriors by casting the demon out of a slave girl. This action incited the whole city, causing a raging mob to literally drag Paul and Silas before the magistrates and accuse them of unlawful acts. The townspeople were furious because this slave girl had brought in money with her psychic readings and now that she was set free, their source of income would dry up.

Could Paul have known this would happen? In hindsight, would Paul be tempted to avoid this situation altogether to keep the peace? Should he have just ignored the girl to avoid trouble? If you knew the outcome, would you have gone through with it?

Satan wants us to live in constant fear. This is one of his sneaky tactics when we engage in spiritual battles like Paul did. However, we must remember that *"greater is He that is in us than he that is in the world"* (1 John 4:4). Satan does not want people to have salvation or freedom from their bondage. He will attack and try to confuse us with doubt and worry.

Acknowledging these tactics helps us to be prepared and reminds us that we are warriors of the Most High God. We possess a power that far exceeds anything Satan can use against us. The Bible assures us that if Jesus is for us, nothing can be against us.

Acts 16 tells us that the magistrates ruled against Paul and Silas. They were beaten with rods and thrown into prison. It's clear from the text that Paul must have been in pain and probably a bit scared, but he never lost sight of his mission. Paul was always on call, 24/7, and understood that God was in control of every circumstance and situation.

God's understanding is infinitely greater than ours. He knew what would happen to Paul and had a plan to use it for His glory. God needed to position Paul to thrive in his moment. He had entrusted Paul with specific gifts and talents, ensuring that Paul could fulfill his divine purpose. In every trial and tribulation, Paul remained steadfast, knowing that God's victory was assured.

So what did Paul do in that situation? Let's read it together, shall we?

Acts 16:25-34 ESV About midnight Paul and Silas were pray-
ing and singing hymns to God, and the prisoners were listening
to them, [26] and suddenly there was a great earthquake, so that
the foundations of the prison were shaken. And immediately all
the doors were opened, and everyone's bonds were unfastened. [27]
When the jailer woke and saw that the prison doors were open,
he drew his sword and was about to kill himself, supposing that
the prisoners had escaped. [28] But Paul cried with a loud voice, "Do
not harm yourself, for we are all here." [29] And the jailer[a] called
for lights and rushed in, and trembling with fear he fell down
before Paul and Silas. [30] Then he brought them out and said,
"Sirs, what must I do to be saved?" [31] And they said, "Believe in
the Lord Jesus, and you will be saved, you and your household."
[32] And they spoke the word of the Lord to him and to all who were
in his house. [33] And he took them the same hour of the night and
washed their wounds; and he was baptized at once, he and all his
family. [34] Then he brought them up into his house and set food
before them. And he rejoiced along with his entire household that
he had believed in God.

At midnight, Paul shifted his focus from his own problems to viewing
his circumstances from God's perspective. He began to pray, worship,
and trust Jesus to bring light to their situation. Paul understood that
he was chosen for this moment to bring glory to God and recognized
that his circumstances could change at any given moment. This was
confirmed when an earthquake occurred, creating an opportunity for
Paul to share Jesus with the jailer. Remarkably, Paul also extended this
opportunity to the jailer's entire family. God is so good!

Most of us would probably shy away from going through such a difficult experience, but what if it were the only way to reach someone for
God's Kingdom? Are we not soldiers in God's army, serving at the pleasure of our King? Have we not been granted eternal life, hope, freedom,
peace, and so much more? Are we not called to lay down our lives for

our brothers and even our enemies? Doesn't God's word instruct us to elevate others above ourselves? Wouldn't this be the least we could do in light of all that God has done for us?

Thrive During Our Pprison Times of Darkness

Paul's time in prison was extensive and provides a rich area for us to explore deeper. By delving into this part of his life, we can learn how to thrive in our own challenging moments, especially when those moments seem dark and bleak. I find this section particularly relatable. My life as both a business owner and pastor often mirrors Paul's experiences. Did you know that Paul was also a business owner? Specifically, he was a tent maker, as mentioned in Acts 18. Like me, Paul found himself in seemingly impossible situations where he had to learn how to thrive against the odds. I call these challenging periods—when we feel immobilized or in a dark, lonely place—our "prison times." During these times, it's crucial to remember that God is always near, desiring for His followers to thrive and perform well for His Kingdom.

One area that frequently binds us is our finances. Many of us strive for financial stability, seeking high-paying jobs while sometimes settling for lower-paying ones to ensure a steady income. We like to know what we'll make each month so that we can plan our lives accordingly. However, when faced with financial uncertainty, our faith and trust in God are challenged, revealing the true strength of our beliefs. Those who live on straight commission are particularly familiar with this struggle. While most of us may not experience physical imprisonment like Paul, many of us may find ourselves in a "financial prison." This kind of constraint can significantly limit what we can do, whether or not greed is a factor.

In these financial prison times, it's vital to remember that God is still with us, providing opportunities to grow and thrive in His service. By examining the life of Paul, we can gain valuable insights into how to navigate our own difficult circumstances with faith and resilience.

God has used my financial prison as a way to teach me the importance of depending not on money but solely on Him. As you read in the motives chapter, where God asked me to conduct my business His way, my wife and I faced financial challenges right from the start. We had to learn to live moment by moment and how to walk victoriously through each of those trying times. Even years later, the financial challenges persist, but God continues to use them to teach me to keep my eyes keenly focused on Him. I share this to illustrate how God has opened my eyes to understanding how to thrive in my moment and trust Him completely.

There are many times in our lives when God's actions make no sense to us. We often struggle to comprehend why He would place us in ostensibly perplexing situations. Remember, the pathway God chooses to mold and shape us into His image is the one He deems best. He knows the areas of our hearts and lives where we are weakest, especially when it comes to bringing Him glory. When we surrender our lives to Him, He will correct any imbalances we may have. In my case, God has used financial scarcity to align my heart and life with His.

Many years later, I have come to understand that God did His greatest work during my prison times. My wife and I have learned to view these trials as opportunities to bring Him glory and flourish. We have become much more sensitive to the Holy Spirit's leading and have come to rest and rejoice in these times. This does not mean it's easy—as it wasn't easy for Paul either—but we can find rest because we know that in Jesus, there is always a way forward. Trusting in His guidance and strength, we can navigate our challenges with the confidence that He will lead us through even the most difficult times. How would we ever know if our faith is real if it hasn't been battle-tested and approved?

I'm sure Paul wasn't pleased when he was in prison. Being confined meant he couldn't be out and about doing ministry. Much like us during our own "prison times," he likely longed for freedom and resented the restraints of his circumstances. These periods are seldom fun and can bring about days of depression, but in the light of eternity, they are only momentary. As God's soldiers, we have a mission that doesn't include dwelling on our problems. Instead, we are to have eyes that see what God is doing and join Him in His work.

Paul exemplified this mindset better than anyone. During his prison times, he didn't focus on the promise of release or cling to false hopes. He thrived in the moment. Not knowing when, or even if, he would be released, Paul chose to pray and worship. He certainly hoped for freedom, but he understood that his life was in God's hands, not his own.

I've often heard it said that if you're in a bad spot, God will make your situation better in time. However, that "better" might mean learning to find contentment even amidst tumultuous storms. Take Paul's imprisonment in Rome, for example. Did he eventually gain his freedom? No, he died a martyr's death. While he was released from prison on several other occasions, his final imprisonment ended in death. Yet, this is not meant to depress you. The point is that Paul thrived in every moment he had, fully understanding that as long as he had breath, he would bring glory to God.

We are called to fix our eyes on Jesus in that same manner, not to be engrossed in our circumstances or problems. By doing so, we can learn to thrive even in our most challenging times, just as Paul did.

George Mueller is one of my faith superheroes! I now see that God has used his life and testimony to help shape mine. If you're not familiar with George Mueller or the facts about his complete dependency on God, I highly recommend reading his autobiography or any other book about him. For those who know me, you'll often hear me talk about George Mueller. He was a man who fully trusted God with his finances and built an empire for Jesus without ever telling anyone about his financial needs.

Reflecting on my life, I realize I have modeled it after George's without even knowing it. George ran an orphanage business, pastored a church, and oversaw a nonprofit that supported missionaries and children. Similarly, I own a small business called Mission Travel Tours that my wife now runs while I consult and step in when needed. I also oversee a nonprofit called Natural Discipleship. We are a ministry that meets needs while training trainers to make multiplying disciples of Jesus, globally.

Like George Mueller, we continue our work as if everything is exactly as it should be, regardless of financial challenges. In reality, whether we're in our prison times or everything seems perfect, it is all as it should be because God is in control, and we are His servants doing His work.

With all of that said, the area where I can best relate to George Mueller is in the realm of finances. God specifically instructed me to trust Him with all my financial needs, just as He did with George, and to refrain from sharing those needs with anyone but Him. This command has been particularly challenging, especially during tight financial periods. Your mind can play tricks on you, leading you to justify why you need to take certain actions to secure money.

In his autobiography, George recounts numerous trials where his financial resources completely dried up. Throughout these times, he demonstrated unwavering trust and constant surrender, believing that God would somehow come through. George stands out as a man of prayer and action. He was always seeking God's guidance in prayer and immediately obedient when that guidance was given.

Like George, I've faced the imprisonment of financial scarcity, often having to operate in ways that differed from what I thought was best. Both George and I have experienced times when God didn't show up according to our preferred timeline. Yet, even when He seems late or our needs aren't fully met, it doesn't mean God doesn't love us. God knows best. He is God, and we are not. This understanding helps us to rest in His sovereignty and trust His perfect timing, no matter the circumstances. When we rest in His provisions and find contentment in His perfect will, every trial we face becomes much easier to endure than if we were to resist Him. Trusting in His faithfulness allows us to navigate our challenges with peace and confidence.

The moral of the story is that God has always shown up and has always been faithful. It has always been on His timing, in His way, ensuring that He is glorified. He has never left me nor forsaken me, and He always acts in a manner that brings glory to His name. George Muller's autobiography masterfully illustrates God's perfect timing and His miraculous ways.

My wife and I have experienced countless miracles, seeing God work in ways that are beyond human comprehension. Perhaps I will share these stories in another book, should the Lord lead. Anyone who has truly surrendered to God and rested in Him can testify to His unwavering goodness and faithfulness. We never have to worry about Him not coming through. We just have to stay consistent and let Him lead, it's our inconsistencies that lead us to despair.

During our "prison times," we are often tempted to implode and give up. My encouragement to you is to do just the opposite! Thrive and conquer everything through surrender. If we stay the course and continue to view our circumstances from God's perspective, our eyes will be opened to new truths we never knew existed. It's a glorious thing!

These prison times are opportunities to do great things for God. Paul wrote Ephesians, Philippians, Colossians, and Philemon while confined in Rome. Can you imagine if we didn't have those amazing epistles in the Bible? Paul never stopped functioning as God's agent of change. He was always on call and ready for duty. Prison was a time for him to reflect on God's goodness and to share that goodness through his writings to the masses.

Paul thrived when things were tough. The greater the trial, the more he leaned on Jesus. Reflect on what Jesus told Paul in 2 Corinthians 12:9 ESV: *"My grace is sufficient for you, for my power is made perfect in weakness. Therefore, I will boast all the more gladly of my weaknesses, so that the power of Christ may rest upon me."* These promises apply to us today as well. During our weakest moments, we should rely on Jesus and thrive through challenges. These are not times for complaint, bitterness, or surrender, but opportunities to achieve great things for God. By spending quiet moments with Him, we learn to hear His voice more clearly and perceive life from His perspective.

Thriving in the present is essential in our walk with God. If you are a true follower of Christ, He is undoubtedly at work in your life right now. There are numerous ministry opportunities surrounding us. God calls us to respond, whether it's through prayer for others—be it family, friends, leaders, or even strangers. We must slow down to observe everything around us and listen to God's voice.

Even when our trials stem from evil against us, God's love permeates them, enabling us to thrive. Now is the time for believers to unite and live holy lives in the moments our King has crafted for us. To achieve this, we must immerse ourselves in God's Word, meditating on His truth. We need to be in constant prayer and communion with God, and we must fellowship with other God-fearing believers. Complaints and boredom have no place in this journey.

We must daily put on the full armor of God and engage in a spiritual battle against Satan. By doing so, we will become high-achieving warriors for Jesus. God made us to win, and together, we can achieve significant victories for Jesus by thriving in every moment.

Alongside the Bible, this book serves as a valuable resource to revisit whenever life's difficulties arise. It offers guidance and reminders on how to navigate your challenges. Additionally, it can be a great resource to share with friends and family who may be facing their own trials and tribulations.

Memorize:

2 Corinthians 12:9 ESV "My grace is sufficient for you, for my power is made perfect in weakness. Therefore I will boast all the more gladly of my weaknesses, so that the power of Christ may rest upon me."

THRIVE IN YOUR MOMENT – Part 2
Talking Points

1. When you gave your life to Jesus, did you feel inspired to thrive in your moment and share the gospel with others?

2. Do you view your circumstances as opportunities to thrive for Jesus? How so?

3. Read Acts 16:16-40 and consider the following questions:
   (a) Why do you think Paul became annoyed with the slave girl?

   (b) What occurred after Paul cast out the spirit?

   (c) What were Paul and Silas doing while in prison, and who heard them?

   (d) What led to Paul and Silas's escape?

4. How did God use Paul's imprisonment for His purposes?

5. Do you truly believe that God is in control of every moment in your life?

6. Do you see yourself as a Warrior for Jesus? Why or why not?

7. When life gets tough, is it easier for you to crumble and complain, or to rise up and thrive? Explain your response.

8. Why do you think Christians often find it difficult to share their faith?

9. Can you recall a time when you felt God's presence during a 'prison' moment in your life? What happened?

10. During challenging times, do you find yourself praying more for your own needs or for others?

[i] Billy Graham - Decision Magazine, January 2016 – online https://billygraham.org/decision-magazine/january-2016/a-message-from-billy-graham-total-surrender/

[ii] Billy Graham - Decision Magazine, January 2016 – online https://billygraham.org/decision-magazine/january-2016/a-message-from-billy-graham-total-surrender/

[iii] Billy Graham - Decision Magazine, January 2016 – online https://billygraham.org/decision-magazine/january-2016/a-message-from-billy-graham-total-surrender/

[iv] Christina Perri - BrainyQuote.com, Xplore Inc, 2017 - online https://www.brainyquote.com/quotes/christina_perri_498043, accessed April 7, 2017

[v] Lucille Ball - BrainyQuote.com, Xplore Inc, 2017 - online https://www.brainyquote.com/quotes/lucille_ball_127076, accessed April 7, 2017

[vi] Ellicott's Commentary for English Readers: Lest he put forth his hand. https://biblehub.com/commentaries/genesis/3-22.htm

[vii] https://www.gotquestions.org/Mosaic-covenant.html

[viii] Kyle Idleman - *Not a Fan: Becoming a completely committed follower of Jesus*. City on a Hill, 2011

[ix] A.W. Tozer provided by: https://www.christianquotes.info/top-quotes/18-beautiful-quotes-holy-spirit/#ixzz4ehrheHND

[x] Word reference study provided by: https://pioneernt.com/2010/02/01/word-study-31-power/

[xi] Word reference study provided by: https://pioneernt.com/2010/02/01/word-study-31-power/

[xii] Oswald Chambers - *my Utmost for His Highest*, Discovery House Publishers, 2006

Keys to being Set Free
Overcoming Hang-ups, Hurts & Addictions

Are you tired of being held captive by hurts, addictions, and hang-ups?

Has your spiritual journey become stagnant and nearly devoid of vitality?

Do you yearn for a life of genuine freedom, where the burden of your current lifestyle no longer determines your current state? Look no further. Keys to Being Set Free is a one-on-one transformative discipleship curriculum you've been looking for.

In this life-changing book, you will embark on a journey guided by biblically balanced principles and practical wisdom. This journey will help addresses the hurts, addictions, and hang-ups that can hinder your spiritual growth and your intimate relationship with the Father. You will discover the keys that will unlock the door to lasting change and restoration.

Order your copy today online at:

BARNES&NOBLE
BOOKSELLERS

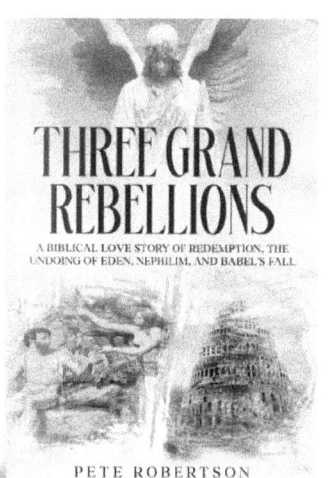

Three Grand Rebellions

A Biblical Love Story of Redemption, the Undoing of Eden, Nephilim and Babel's Fall

In the intricate tapestry of existence, woven within the threads of history and eternity, lies a thin line, often unseen, but holding fast the narrative of the cosmos. "Three Grand Rebellions: A Bible Love Story of Redemption, the Undoing of Eden, Nephilim, and Babel's Fall" is an invitation to embark on a profound journey, a quest to illuminate the subtle and profound intricacies of divine design that have too often lain concealed in the shadows of our understanding.

The book will piece together a mosaic of truths that showcase how Christ's obedience achieved even more than we had previously understood by answering the following questions:

- How does God's redemption thread run through the Bible?
- How did Jesus reverse the curse of the Three Grand Rebellions?
- Who is the assembly of the Divine Council?
- How Did descendants of the Nephilim survive the flood?
- Why is it important for believers to take back land by discipleship?

Discover the answer to those questions today,

Order your copy today online at:

amazon

BARNES&NOBLE
BOOKSELLERS

www.ingramcontent.com/pod-product-compliance
Lightning Source LLC
Chambersburg PA
CBHW051304120626
46547CB00015B/2088